ISBN 978-2-35328-091-9
Dépot légal 3e trimestre 2012
et 2e trimestre 2016

Maps:
TOP25 N°3630 OT and N°3531 ET

Laurence Dadillon

CHAMONIX-MONT-BLANC

Mountain Range & Valley

The must-hikes

New edition

Éditinter Éditions
Chamonix-Randos

Foreword

Chamonix attracts tourists from around the world, mountaineers, hikers or just families, it is perhaps this blend which makes the third most visited natural site in the world still as authentic and user friendly.

The Mont-Blanc mountain range is 30 km long by 10km wide, 28 summits of more than 4,000 m, the rooftop of Europe (4,810 m), set on the Italian and Swiss borders. Thanks to its ski lifts, the capital of mountaineering allows to reduce the time of approach and to reach the high-mountain and its glaciers.

Each hike will allow you to contemplate exceptional landscapes and their mythical summits, with the Mont-Blanc mountain range in the background.

The variety of routes will make you go alongside various alpine floors: forests, high mountain pastures and Hérens cows, granite rock faces and the sérac waterfalls, high mountain lakes, marmots and ibex…

The hiking routes selected in this guide book were all reported from hikes made by the author, for more than 10 years. The hikes are classified by sector then by level of difficulty: **Easy**, **Hiker**, **Experienced Hiker**.

The distance travelled on the mountain not being significant, the hiking time is specified excluding breaks for an average walker, as well as the accumulated positive or negative difference in height.

For each hike, it is recommended to dedicate one half-day minimum and for the most part one whole day, to take advantage of exceptional sites and panoramas.

In the continuity of the "day" hikes the author suggests her **Tour of the Mont-Blanc** on the mythical path of the GR TMB.

Finally, an introduction to the glacial hikes under the supervision of a mountain guide and to the vastness of the wild spaces they propose.

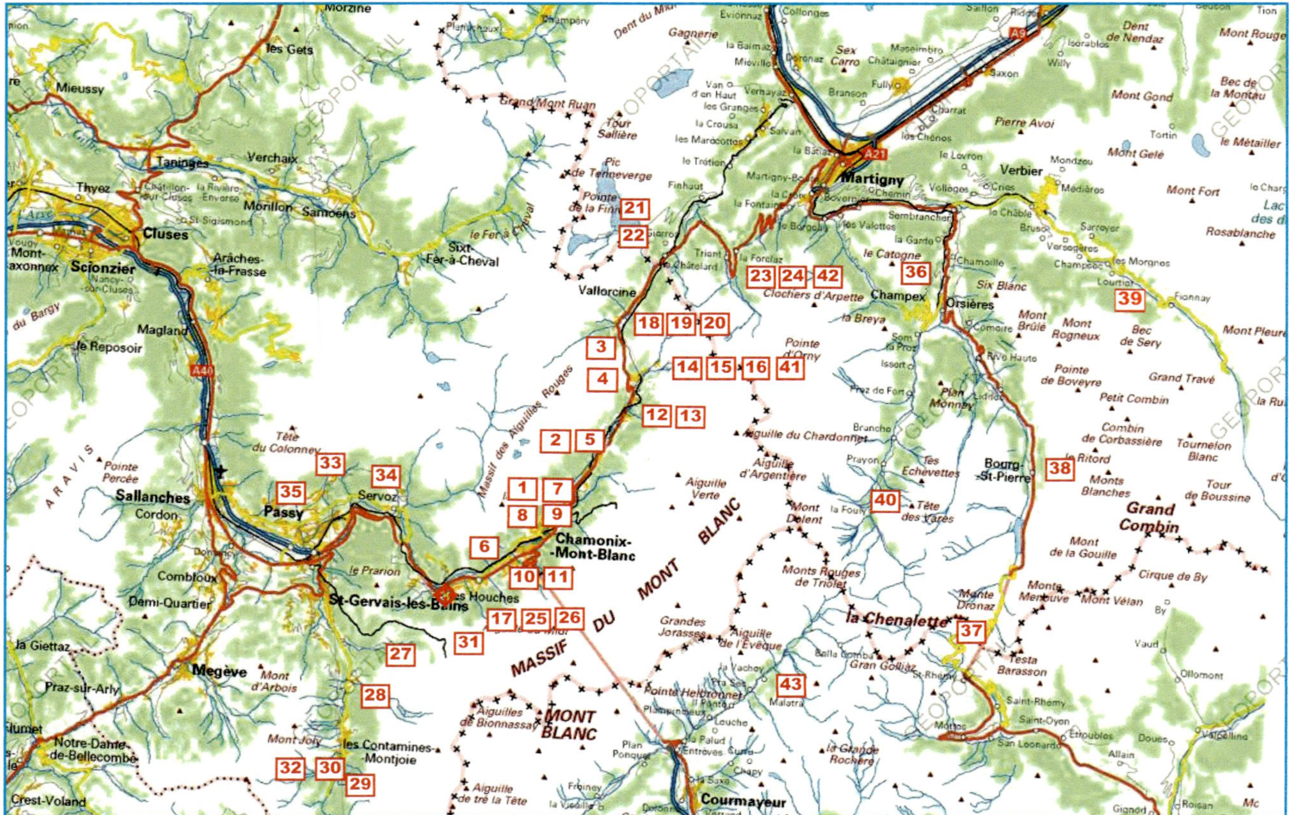

MONT BLANC
MASSIF DU MONT BLANC
Chamonix-Mont-Blanc
Martigny
Courmayeur
Grand Combin
la Chenalette
Verbier
Orsières
Champex
Vallorcine
Bourg-St-Pierre
St-Gervais-les-Bains
les Houches
Servoz
Passy
Sallanches
Cluses
Scionzier
Megève
Combloux
Samoëns
Morillon
Taninges
Sixt-Fer-à-Cheval
les Contamines-Montjoie
Clochers d'Arpette
Aiguille du Chardonnet
Aiguille d'Argentière
Aiguille Verte
Grandes Jorasses
Aiguilles de Bionnassay
Massif des Aiguilles Rouges
Pointe Helbronner
1 2 3 4 5 6 7 8 9 10 11 12 13 14 15 16 17 18 19 20 21 22 23 24 25 26 27 28 29 30 31 32 33 34 35 36 37 38 39 40 41 42 43

SUMMARY

ONE DAY HIKES

Title of the Hike	Difficulty	Hiking time	Cumulated positive difference in height	Page
VALLEY OF CHAMONIX				
01. Balcon Sud (Traversée Planpraz/Flégère)	Easy	2h	Balcony	13
02. Lac Blanc from The Index	Easy	3h	889m	15
03. Lac Blanc from Col des Montets	Hiker	4h	Balcony	17
04. Lac Blanc from Tré-Les-Champs	Hiker	5h	933m	21
05. Lacs Noirs, Lac Cornu	Hiker	3h	194m	23
06. Refuge Bel Lachat, Aiguillette des Houches, Chalets Chailloux	Hiker	5h	805m	25
07. Refuge Bel Lachat et Aiguillette des Houches via le Brévent	Hiker	5h	183m	27
08. Pont d'Arlevé	Hiker	5h30	771m	29
09. Grand Balcon Nord	Hiker	3h	530m	31
10. Chalet des Pyramides	Hiker	2h30	470m	33
11. La Jonction	Experienced Hiker	6h30 à 7h	1165m	35
12. Viewpoint of the Argentière Glacier	Easy	2h	362m	37
13. La Pendant, Le Chapeau and Le Lavancher Chalets	Easy	3h	---	39
14. Refuge Albert 1er	Hiker	3h30	550m	41
15. Col de Balme, Croix de fer, Col des Posettes	Hiker	3h30	346m	43
16. Col de Balme, Croix de fer, Vallorcine or Le Buet	Hiker	3h	157m	45
17. Le Prarion andt Mont-Lachat	Hiker	3h30	585m	47

VALLEY OF VALLORCINE

18. Refuge de Loriaz	Hiker	4h	680m	**49**
19. Refuge de la Pierre à Bérard	Hiker	3h40	584m	**51**
20. Tré-Les-Eaux Valley	Hiker	5h	660m	**53**
21. Dinosaurs Tracks	Hiker	5h	540m	**55**
22. Refuge de Loriaz, Col de la Terrasse	Experienced Hiker	6h	685m	**57**
23. Fenêtre de l'Arpette	Experienced Hiker	6h30	1139m	**59**
24. Fenêtre de l'Arpette to Champex ; Champex to Col de la Forclaz by Bovine	Experienced Hiker	2 days	D1:1139m D2: 589m	**61**

VALLEY OF BIONNASSAY/LES CONTAMINES-MONTJOIE

25. Nid d'Aigle - Baraque des Rognes - Glacier de Bionnassay	Hiker	4h30	306m	**63**
26. Col du Tricot from Bellevue	Hiker	4h	520m	**65**
27. Col du Tricot from Bionnassay	Hiker	4h30	700m	**67**
28. Truc and Miage Chalets	Hiker	3h30	720m	**69**
29. Jovet Lakes	Hiker	5h30	980m	**71**
30. The Aiguille de Roselette ; Col du Mont Joly pass	Hiker	5h	450m	**73**
31. Nid d'Aigle - Tête Rousse refuge	Hiker	4h	795m	**75**
32. Mont Joly mountain range	Experienced Hiker	6h30 à 7h	1045m	**77**

SECTOR OF ANTERNE

33. Col d'Anterne, Lake Pormenaz	Hiker	5h	889m	**79**
34. Lake Pormenaz from Servoz	Hiker	6h15	1080m	**81**
35. From Varan to Platé via the Col de Barmerousse pass	Experienced Hiker	7h	1356m	**83**

SWISS MOUNTAINSIDE

36. Cabane d'Orny	Hiker	4h	650m	85
37. Fenêtre Lakes	Hiker	4h30	832m	87
38. Cabane de Valsorey (2 days)	Experienced Hiker	2 days	D1:1340m	89
39. Cabane Panossière	Hiker	5h30	785m	93
40. Col du Basset (La Fouly)	Hiker	3h15	871m	95
41. Cabane des Grands from lthe Col de Balme pass (Le Tour)	Hiker	3h30	Balcony	97
42. Cabane des Grands from the Col de La Forclaz	Hiker	4h	590m	99

ITALIAN MOUNTAINSIDE

43. Entre-Deux-Sauts	Hiker	4h30	841m	101

TOUR OF THE MONT-BLANC	Experienced Hiker	6 jours		102

THE GLACIAL HIKES

Haute Vallée Blanche crossing 109

Refuge de Leschaux 111

Refuge d'Argentière 113

Tour de la Mer de Glace 115

Dômes de Miage,central summit 119

The 3 Passes 123

Grand Paradis 127

PRACTICAL TIPS 129

USEFUL INFORMATION 131

ONE-DAY HIKES

Hiking in the mountain requires a good physical preparation and adequate equipment.
Always inquire about weather conditions before leaving and keep in mind that the weather can change abruptly.
Leave early to avoid high clouds which arrive during the day or mid-afternoon thunderstorms.
The indicated schedules include the walking time but not the time for stops (breaks for picnics, drinks, photos, observations, etc.). On average, one should allow 1 hour to go up a positive elevation of 300 m. To take advantage of landscapes or of sites, one can dedicate a day for every hike.
The hikes were classified into three difficulty levels: **Easy**, **Hiker**, **Experienced Hiker**. In all cases, remember that these are altitude hikes.
Easy: hiking time 3 hours max or elevation gain 500 m max.
Hiker: hiking time 3-6 hours max or elevation gain 500 to 1,000 m, physically fit.
Experienced hiker: hiking time > 6 hours or positive elevation gain > 1,000 m, very fit, good mountain experience. The routes are marked by signs, paint marks or cairns.

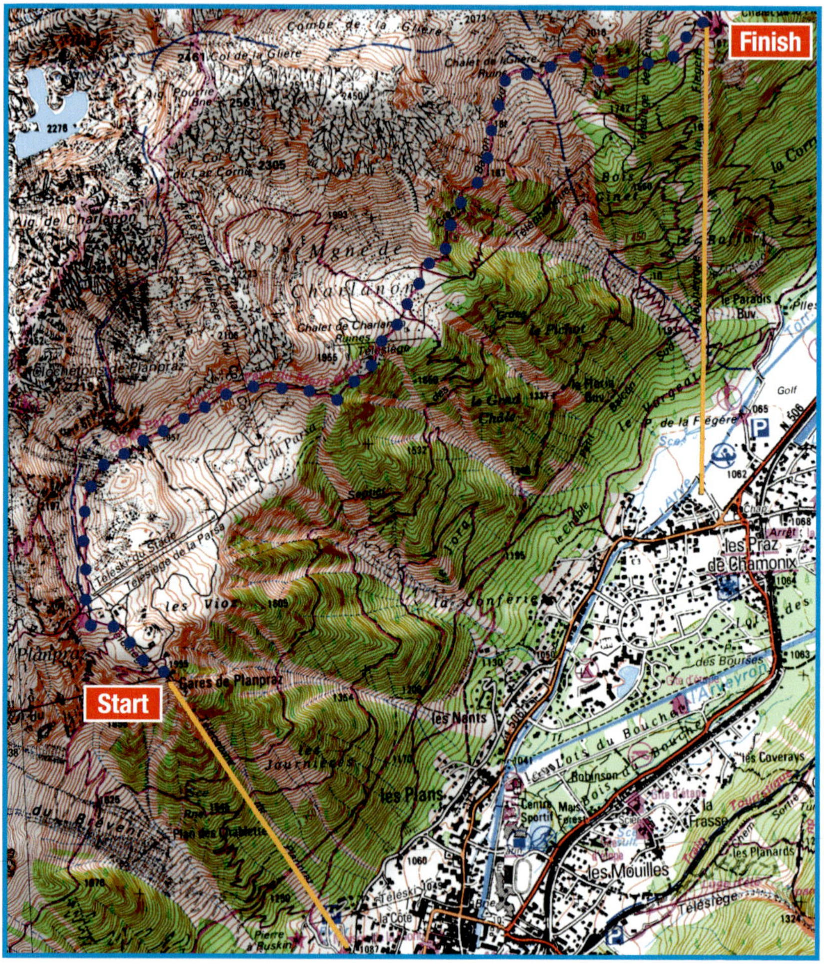

Altitude: 1,999 m Start Planpraz
Level: Easy
Time: 2 hours
Elevation: Balcony
IGN 3630 OT map or Pays du Mont-Blanc hiking map (A1 Rando editions)
Access: Brévent cable car parking lot in Chamonix (paying).

01 I Balcon Sud (Planpraz / Flégère Crossing)

A superb crossing on a sunny balcony that you can do as a family in half a day (preferably in the morning) which offers an unobstructed view of the Mont-Blanc mountain range all along the way.

At the ticket office, take a one way ticket to Planpraz and return to Flégère. Take the Planpraz cable car. On the way out, take the trail that rises above the cable car to the chalet "Altitude 2000".
Leave to the left the path which takes you up to the Brévent pass and take the path on your right towards La Flégère. The trail follows part of the route of the Grand Balcon Sud. It goes easily along a ledge through old pastures. One joins the Charlanon valley (1,820 m) halfway where a spring flows near a small cottage in ruins.

Ignore the path on the left that leads to Lake Cornu and the one on the right that goes down to Chamonix, and continue the Grand Balcon Sud. Ignore the path to the right, which goes to the Chalet Flégère, and continue the Grand Balcon Sud path towards the ruins of the Chalet de la Glière (Pays du Mont-Blanc Tour). You then pass through the Glière valley, then the forest floor before reaching the cable car station of La Flégère (1,877 m). From the Viewpoint, the view embraces the entire Mont-Blanc mountain range, the Tour, Argentière and Mer de Glace glaciers. There is generous flora and blueberries in season.
Take the Flégère cable car, which takes you back to the Praz.
Praz Flégère link to Chamonix center by bus in July/August.
This Grand Balcon Sud crossing can be achieved in one direction or the other. However, for those who do not know Chamonix, I recommend as proposed because before starting, you can take the Brévent cable car (preferably in the morning before the arrival of high clouds), which is at the exit of the Planpraz intermediate station. In this case, at the ticket office, ask for a one way to Brévent and return Brévent Planpraz plus a return to Flégère.
The Brévent (2,525 m) has a magnificent viewpoint over the Mont-Blanc mountain range, its peaks and glaciers. The view also extends to the Fiz massif. Viewpoint.
Back at Planpraz you can also admire the many hang gliders that soar from the take-off area.

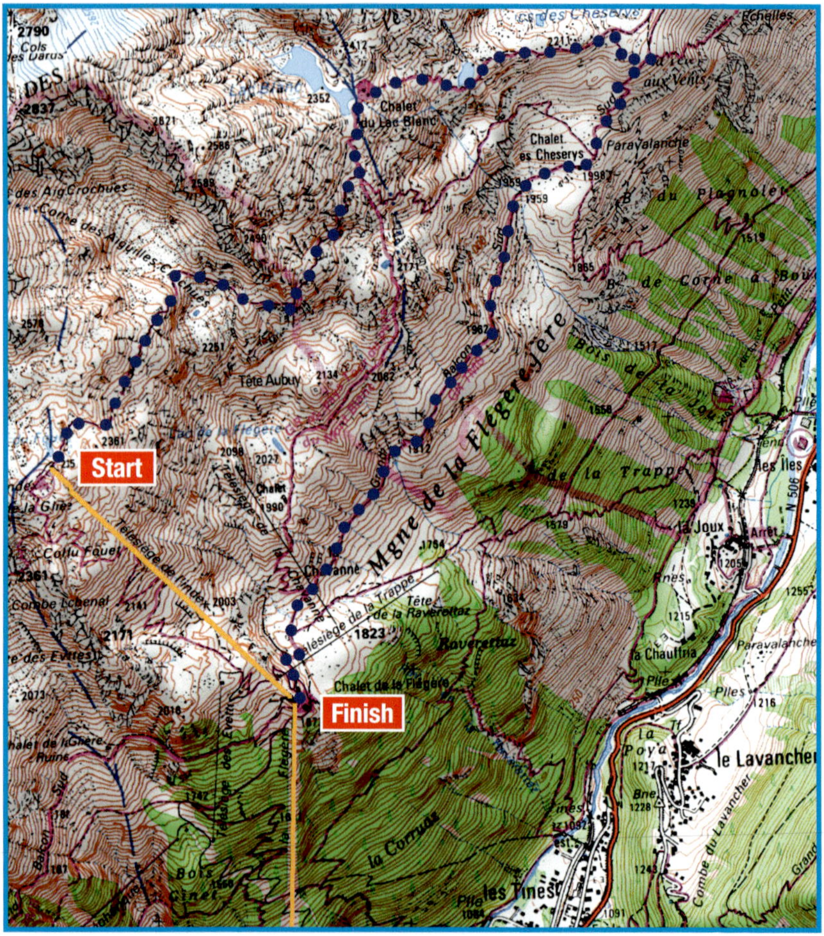

Altitude: 2,350 m Lac Blanc Refuge
Level: Easy
Time: 3 hours
Elevation: Crossing by balcony from Index (2,385 m), descent 473 m
IGN 3630 OT map or Pays du Mont-Blanc hiking map (A1 Rando Editions)
Access: La Flégère cable car parking lot in Les Praz.
Guarded refuge from mid-June to mid-September: 04 50 53 49 14 (40 beds)

02 I Lac Blanc from the Index

The Lac Blanc is the unavoidable hike of Chamonix. A family hike with no elevation, all along the route, postcard panoramas of most of the Mont-Blanc mountain range. A great show is on the snowy peaks guaranteed: Mont-Blanc, Aiguille du Midi, the Mer de Glace, the Drus, the Tour and Argentière glaciers.

There are many routes leading up to Lac Blanc. They are also quite busy. This hike is a less travelled route than the one starting from the arrival station of the La Flégère cable car.

At the ticket office, take a oneway ticket to La Flégère-Index and a return to La Flégère.

Take the cable car of La Flégère then the Index chairlift.

The trail goes down to the right of the Index chairlift and passes next to the small lake of Le Fouet. It is not uncommon to see snowfields that delight children. The trail on the mountainside is a permanent lookout on the Mont-Blanc chaine. One joins the refuge in 1h20.

In the summer, the thawed Lac Blanc (actually two joined lakes), is a turquoise colour. Keep to the right of the first lake for a picnic on the shores of the second lake, which is quieter. Some brave have a (quick) dip in the glacial lake. The Yellow-billed choughs (large crows) watch out for the crumbs. To go back, take the path signposted "Lacs des Chéserys" to the left.

The path descends to the southern shores of the Chéserys lake (2,211 m) by taking a short and easy ladder that allows the crossing of rock aplomb.

Following the path, you can see the other lakes set on a wide terrace that stretches halfway up the Aiguilles Rouges. You then come to a fork. You are at the heart of the scenery: A 180° panorama on the Mont-Blanc and its mythical summits, Aiguille du Tour, Aiguille du Chardonnct, Aiguille Verte, Drus, the Mer de Glace, the Jorasses and the Mont-Blanc.

You are sure to see Ibex along the way.

Take a right onto the TMB, trail, which leads to the Chéserys chalet (1,998 m) and then to the hut of La Chavanne. A short climb (unpleasant) takes you back to the top station cable car of La Flégère (1,877 m).

Take the cable car back to the parking lot.

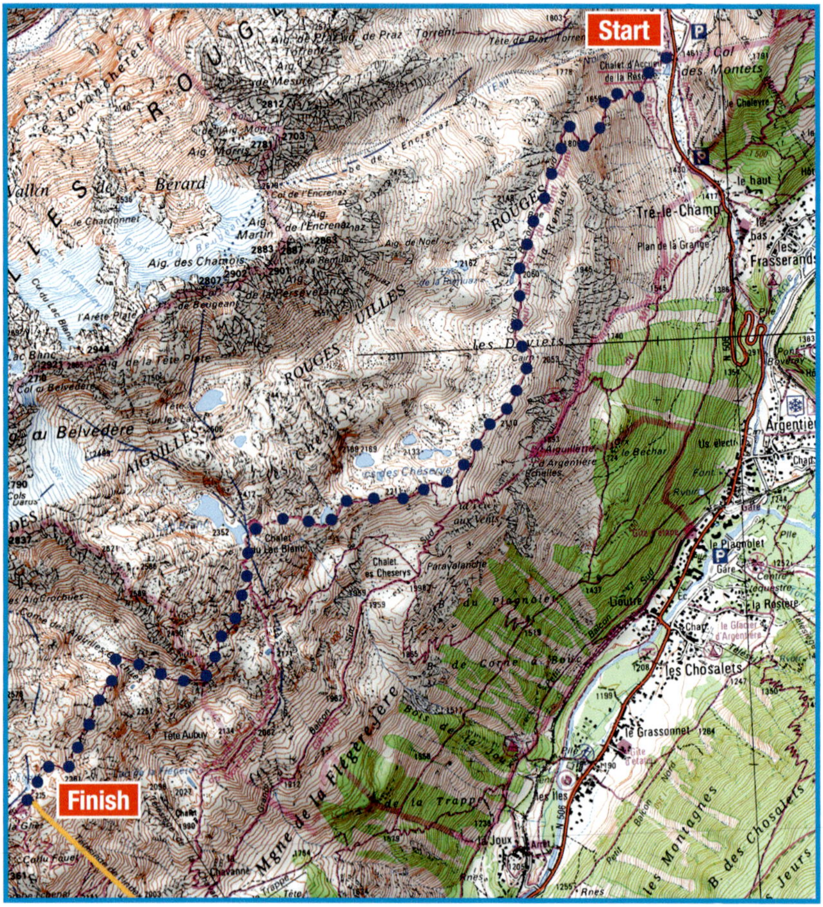

Altitude: 2,350 m Lac Blanc Refuge, 2,385 m Index
Level: Hiker
Time: Ascent Lac Blanc 3 hours + Crossing to Index 1 hour
Elevation: Ascent Lac Blanc 889 m
IGN 3630 OT map or Pays du Mont-Blanc hiking map (A1 Rando Editions)
Access: The Col des Montets parking, after Argentière (N 506)
Bus # 21 Chamonix-Col des Montets
Return to Les Praz by the Index chairlift + La Flégère cable car.

03 I Lac Blanc from the Col des Montets

The Lac Blanc is the unavoidable hiking day of Chamonix. Throughout the route, you will see postcard panoramas of the Mont-Blanc range. From the Col de Balme to the Col de Voza, a great show is to be expected on the snowy peaks: The du Tour and Argentière glaciers, the Drus, the Mer de Glace, the Aiguille du Midi, the Mont-Blanc...

There are many routes up to Lac Blanc. It is also very busy. The proposed hike is a less used crossing, quieter and away from the crowd, starting from the Col des Montets parking lot.

A bus allows you to get to the Col des Montets between late June and early September. It leaves at 9.00 am from the Place du Mont-Blanc in Chamonix, and arrives at 9:30 am at the Col des Montets.

The return is made by the Index chairlift and la Flégère cable car. The best way is to park your car at Les Praz, at La Flégère parking, and buy your return ticket before the hike and catch the bus at 9:00 am from Les Praz/La Flégère bus stop that drops you at 9:30 am at the Col des Montets.

At the Col des Montets (1,461 m), take the trailhead behind the Botanical reception chalet of the Aiguilles Rouges reserve, the trail rises quickly in zig-zags..

Within 30 minutes, you have a great view of the Tour and Argentière glaciers on one side and on the other the Vallorcine Valley.

In 1h45, there is a 180° panorama on the Mont-Blanc and its mythical summits, Aiguille du Tour, Aiguille du Chardonnet, Aiguille Verte and the Drus.

In 2 hours, you will reach a fork where you leave the path towards Argentière/Flégère to follow that of Lac Blanc/Lacs des Chéserys. You are in the heart of the postcard, the view is always the same with the Jorasses and the Mont-Blanc to boot.

Ibex assured along the way.

One can see the Chéserys lakes on the right, set on a wide terrace that stretches halfway up the Aiguilles Rouges. The path leads down to the southern shores of the Chéserys lake. From the lake, one can see among the overhanging rocks, the Lac Blanc refuge and the rest of the route.

One joins the shelter within 20 minutes after the last climb, taking a short and easy way that enables to cross rock aplomb.

In the summer, the thawed Lac Blanc (actually two joined glacial lakes) is turquoise in colour. Keep to the right of the first lake for a picnic on the shores of the second lake, which is quieter. Some brave take a (quick!) bath in the lake. The yellow-billed choughs (large crows) watch out for the crumbs.

Go back on your steps and turn to the right of the refuge where a path is signposted "L'Index". You reach the top of the Index chairlift in one hour by an overhanging path, still with an extraordinary panorama of the Mont-Blanc.

Take the chairlift and cable car downhill from la Flégère to return to the parking lot. From the Lac Blanc, I do not recommend the direct return by the path signposted "La Flégère" (1h10) which is a true hikers highway in both directions (up and down from the cable car of La Flégère to Lac Blanc). For those who would do this hike outside peak season and when the bus to the Col des Montets still works, or for those not wishing to use the cable car or chairlifts (Index/ la Flégère), for the return journey from the Lac Blanc, you can return to the Col des Montets by the same route (2h10) or by Tré-les-Champs (2h10 up to Tré-les-Champs).

The return by Tré-les-Champs follows the same path from the Lac Blanc and then at the level of the Chéserys lakes, ignore the path taken on the way up on the left (towards the Col des Montets) and take the one to the right towards Tré-les-Champs. At the level of the Aiguillette d'Argentière (1,893 m), you go over granite cliffs thanks to a passage (a handrail on the rock and 2 ladders). Continue the descent through a larch forest towards Plan de la Grange and Tré-le-Champ-le-Haut. The path on the left joins the reception chalet of the Col des Montets.

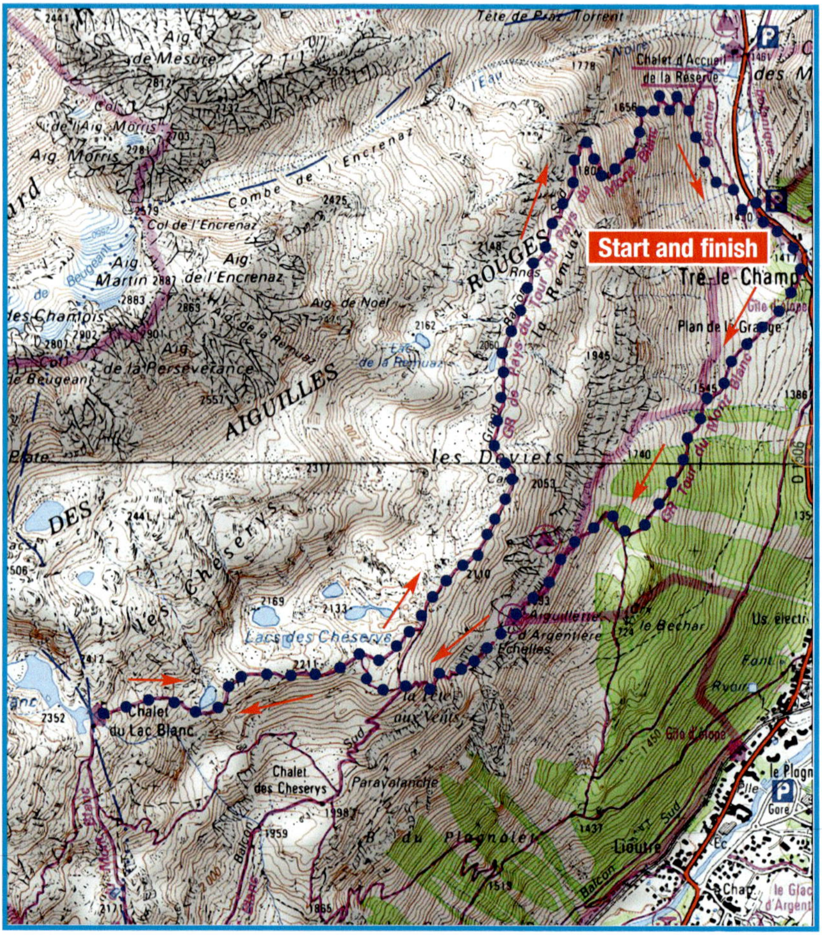

Altitude: 2,350 m at Lac Blanc refuge
Level: Hiker
Time: 2h45 min there, 2h15 min back
Elevation: 933 m ascent from Tré-Les-Champs (1,417 m)
Map: IGN 3630 OT
Access: Tré-Les-Champs parking lot right after Argentières (N506) and just after the village of Tré-Les-Champs, to the left or to the right (two parking lots)

04 I Lac Blanc from Tré-Les-Champs

Lac Blanc is the must-do Chamonix hike. All along the way there are postcard panoramas of the Mont Blanc mountain chain, almost in its entirety. From Col de Balme pass to Col de Voza pass, there is a great show of perspective along the snowy summits: the Tour and Argentière glaciers, the Aiguille du Dru, the Mer de Glace, the Aiguille du Midi, Mont Blanc and more.

This circular hike starts at the Tré-Les-Champs parking lot and returns by the Col des Montets pass. For those who aren't afraid to take a few ladders, climbing up at Tré-Les-Champs is easier than going from Col des Montets (Hike 3). It's my preferred Lac Blanc itinerary!
The path starts from the parking lot on the left-hand side when you're coming from Argentière. It rises through a thick forest of larch trees with blueberries on the right and gorgeous views of the glacier, the village of Tour, and the Grands-Montets on the left.

After 45 min, you'll get to a fork in the road. You'll pass the trail to the left that descends back to Argentière and head to the right towards "Aiguillette d'Argentière/Lacs du Chéserys/Lac Blanc." After 1h15min, you'll arrive at the Aiguillette of Argentière (1,893 m) and the first ladders that allow you to cross the rocky ridge of the granite cliffs. After 30 min you'll reach the end of the ladders. In total there are around ten ladders, each taking between 3-10 meters. At around 2 hours, you'll meet back up with the pathway coming from the Col des Montets on the right with a 180° panoramic view of the Mont Blanc mountain chain and its mythical summits: the Aiguille du Tour, the Aiguille du Chardonnet, the Aiguille Verte and the Aiguille du Dru. Leave behind the route towards "Argentière/Flégère" and head instead towards "Lac Blanc / Lacs des Chéserys." Check out Hike 3 for the next steps of the itinerary up to the Lac Blanc refuge, where you can have a picnic.
For the way back, take the same route you came in with. It will take you about 30 min to reach the Chéserys lakes. Then, take the path on the left marked "Col des Montets" (leaving behind the path on the right marked "Argentière / Tré-Les-Champs / Chalets des Chéserys/ La Flégère"). After about 1 hour (from the refuge), you'll arrive at a ledge with a stone cairn called "La Mare." This is the Aiguilles Rouges area, a magnificent and exotic natural reserve with views over the village of Balme and the Tour glacier. At about 1h20 min, you'll start the steep and winding descent towards the Col des Montets pass with views over Vallorcine and Switzerland. You'll immediately notice the Col des Montets parking lot below you to the left, and on the right you'll see the Tré-les-Champs parking lot. Nevertheless, it's still quite a hike. At 1 h45min, take a break and look out over the Tour and Argentière glaciers. At 2h10 min, you'll pass a trail to your left and continue on towards the Col des Montets reception chalet. Take the trail to the right to head to the Tré-Les-Champs parking lot.

Valley of Chamonix

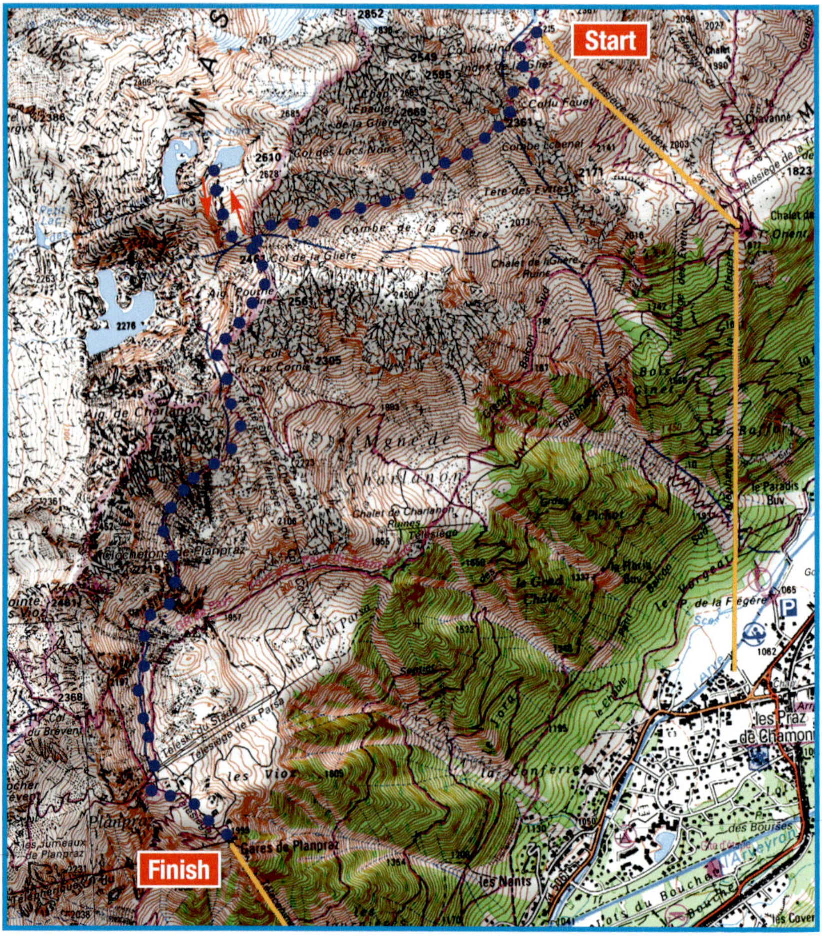

Altitude: 2,534 m Lacs Noirs
Level: Hiker
Time: 3 hours (1hour 30 min for the Lacs Noirs)
Elevation: Ascent 194 m, Descent 536 m
IGN 3630 OT map or Pays du Mont-Blanc hiking map (A1 Rando editions)
Access: La Flégère cable car parking lot in Les Praz.
Return by de Planpraz cable car to Chamonix Brévent Parking lot.

05 I Lacs Noirs, Lac Cornu

A hike in a rocky landscape to three mountain lakes in the Aiguilles Rouges Reserve. Because of their altitude and orientation, these lakes remain bordered by snowfields even in the summer.

At the ticket office, take a one-way ticket to Flégère + Index and a return to Planpraz. Take the Flégère cable car and the Index chairlift (2,385 m).
Upon arrival of the Index chairlift, the trail descends to the left and heads towards the Col de Glière, take this direction. The trail runs along L'Épaule de La Glière du Col de Fouet (2,340 m) below the Index top station right up to the col de La Glière (2,461 m). The trail is little used because the "classic" route and one generally described for the lakes, leaves from the middle station of Planpraz.
The trail runs among rubble stones, surrounded by a rocky landscape, with almost nonexistent vegetation, which gives one an impression of being in high mountains.

A good climb before reaching the Col de la Glière (2,461 m, Cairn), where snowfields often remain.
At the Col de la Glière, the trail to the Lacs Noirs is on the right (yellow marking on the rocks).
You can picnic preferably by the Lacs Noirs (two lakes: Upper Lac Noir and Lower Lac Noir) from where the view is superb. Moreover, by their altitude and their situation, the lakes can remain snowy part of the summer, which adds to the high mountain atmosphere. The view stretches far on the other side, especially on the rock barrier of the Fiz.
Come back on your steps to the Col de la Glière then turn to the right and continue on the path to the Col du Lac Cornu (2,414 m, Cairn). You will see the lake below (2,286 m).
Stay on the path towards Planpraz (1,998 m) (Leave on your left the path going down to Charlanon). The view of the Mont-Blanc chaine becomes more conventional but still beautiful.
Take the Planpraz gondola that takes you back to the Brévent parking lot in Chamonix. A bus runs from Chamonix Centre to Les Praz-Flégère in July/ August.
For those who wish to join the cable car top station of La Flégère from Planpraz, add two hours by taking the Planpraz Flégère crossing by the Grand Balcon Sud (see hike # 1). It then reaches the cable car to La Flégère in Les Praz from where one left in the morning. In this case, take a return ticket to La Flégère.

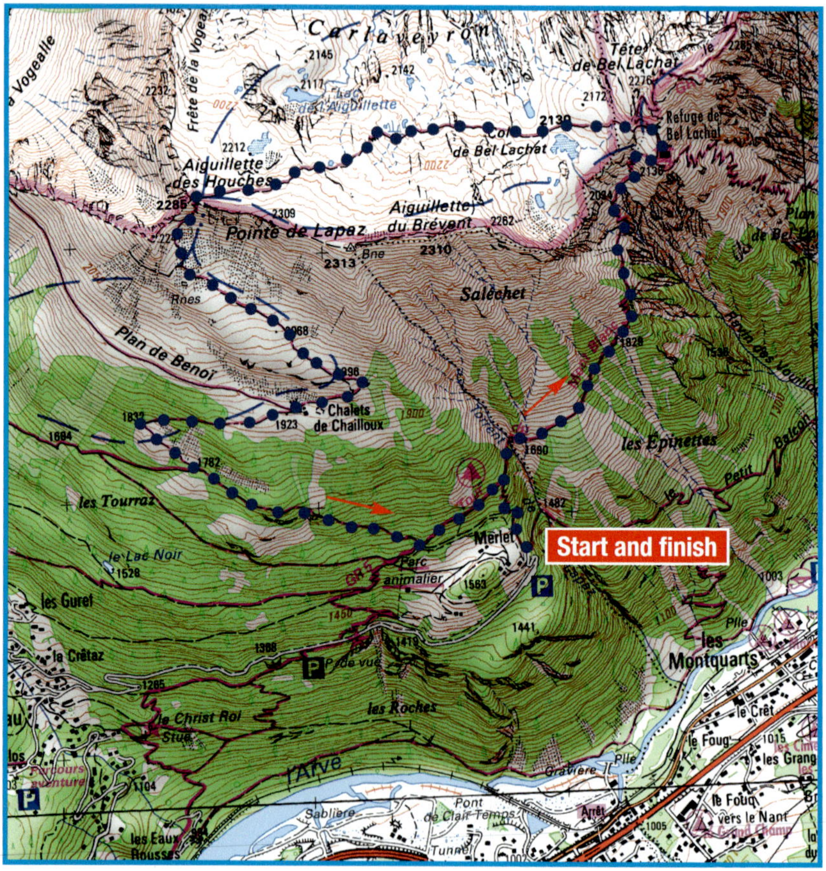

Altitude: 1,480 m to 2,285 m
Level: Hiker
Time: 5 hours
Elevation: Ascent 805 m, Descent 805 m
IGN 3531 ET map or Pays du Mont-Blanc hiking map (A1 Rando Editions)
Access: Parking Merlet Animal Park, Les Houches (http://www.parcdemerlet.com)
From Les Houches, cross the N 205, the Arve and the railway line, on the right take a small winding road that climbs towards the Parc Merlet; road that ends in a dirt road.
Bel Lachat refuge kept from mid June to mid-September: 04 50 53 43 23 (30 beds).

06 I Refuge Bel Lachat, Aiguillette des Houches, Chalets Chailloux

A well observed elevation hike to the Bel Lachat refuge. After crossing wild grasslands of the Carlaveyron reserve, a 360° view awaits you from the Aiguillette des Houches, facing the Mont-Blanc and the Bossons glacier.

From the parking lot, go up towards the park entrance where you will see ibex, chamois, marmots... in semi-freedom. Take the path on the left signposted "refuge Bel Lachat" which goes up in the forest along the park fence.
After 15 minutes, leave the trail to the left that goes towards the Chalets des Chailloux which will be taken on the return journey and continue the climb winding through the forest towards the refuge (TMB route).

After 30 minutes, cross the Lapaz stream and then take a rocky trail equipped with a handrail and some steps. The trail runs between the spruce trees and gives a stunning view of the Glacier des Bossons and the Aiguilles de Chamonix.
After 2h15, and a steep climb one reaches the Bel Lachat refuge (2,136 m) and its lovely terrace with panoramic views of the Valley of Chamonix and the Mont-Blanc range.
After a well deserved rest, take the path above the refuge on the left towards the Aiguillette des Houches (on the right is the path going to the Brévent). The trail full of cairns, then goes gently up amongst the short and wet grass of the Carlaveyron Nature Reserve, which is a vast wilderness.
After 3h15, one reaches the Aiguillette des Houches (2,285 m), the place is conducive for a picnic with a wonderful view facing the Mont-Blanc and at its feet the Bossons glacier.
For the return loop, continue in the direction of the Pierre Blanche on the path which goes down on a tight ridge, with views over the valley of Servoz, the Fiz rocks and on the horizon Aravis, the Bauges and the Beaufortin.
A little before reaching the Pierre Blanche forest, turn left and take the path that leads to the pasture toward the Chalets de Chailloux. The pasture of the Chalets de Chailloux (1,923 m) is favorable for a nap whilst still facing the impressive Mont-Blanc, before starting the last part of the descent (45 min), by a forest trail which joins the Merlet park.

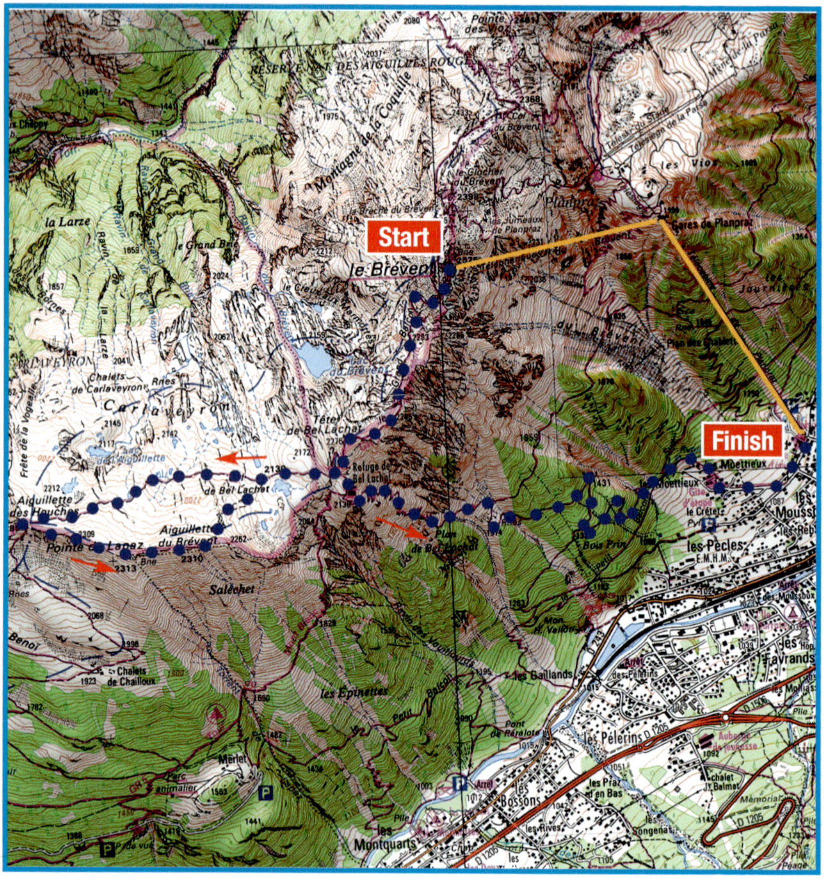

Altitude: 2,525 m to 1,090 m
Level: Hiker
Time: 5 hours (including 2 hours for Brévent-Aiguillette des Houches and 2 hours for Bel Lachat refuge to Chamonix)
Elevation: Ascent 183 m, Descent 1,435 m
IGN map 3630 OT or Pays du Mont-Blanc hiking map (A1 Rando Editions)
Access: Brévent cable car parking lot in Chamonix.
Bel Lachat refuge kept from mid June to mid-September: 04 50 53 43 23

07 I Refuge Bel Lachat, Aiguillette des Houches via le Brévent

A downhill hike from the top of the Brévent. After crossing the wild grasslands reserve of Carlaveyron, the Aiguillette crest (Les Houches and Brévent) offers stunning views of the Mont-Blanc and the Bossons glacier.

This hike enables you to go to the Aiguillette des Houches without the elevation of uphill hiking N°5, which leaves the Merlet Animal Park. By taking the Brévent cable car this hike is a great descent.

At the ticket office, take a one-way ticket Planpraz + Brévent. Take the Planpraz gondola then the Brévent cable car (2,525 m).

On arrival, enjoy the view of the Mont-Blanc range, its peaks and glaciers. The view also extends to the Fiz massif. Viewpoint indicator.

From the arrival station of the Brévent cable car, turn left towards lake Brévent and the Bel Lachat refuge.

After several sharp bends, one overlooks Lake Brévent. Ignore the path on the right towards the lake and proceed towards the refuge. Leave the path on the left which leads to the refuge and continue towards the Col de Bel Lachat and the Aiguillette des Houches.

The cairne trail then goes along in a gentle climb among the short and wet grass of the Carlaveyron Nature Reserve, a vast wilderness. Within 2 hours one reaches the Aiguillette des Houches (2,285 m) which has a wonderful view facing the Mont-Blanc and the Bossons glacier at its feet. Continue along the crest path, (which is not indicated), towards the Pointe de Lapaz (2,313 m), after making a U-turn on the left at 135°. You can picnic on the trail between the peaks Aiguillette des Houches and Aiguillette du Brévent.

From the Aiguillette du Brévent, you reach the path taken in the morning upstream of the Bel Lachat pass. Retrace your steps to the pass and then continue to the refuge (on the left you leave the trail taken in the morning which goes back to the Brévent).

You reach the Bel Lachat refuge (2,136 m) and a lovely terrace with panoramic views of the Chamonix valley and the Mont-Blanc massif.

From the refuge, go down into the valley by the trail on the far left towards Planpraz. On the right, one leaves the TMB path that leads down to Les Houches, Parc Merlet which winds its way down the valley of Bel Lachat which dominates Chamonix. After an hour, leave the trail on your left towards Planpraz and continue on the right. After numerous bends in the forest, you reach the heights of Chamonix, Les Moussoux and La Mollard before returning to the Planpraz gondola parking lot.

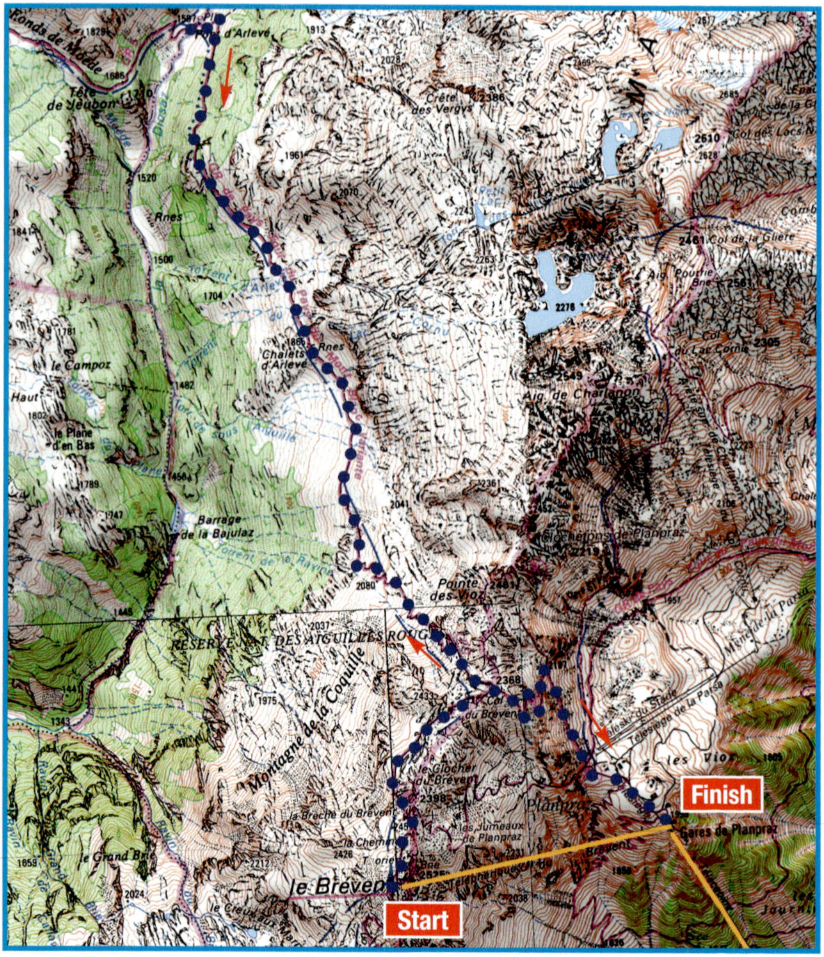

Altitude: 2,525 m (Brévent) to 1,597 m (Pont d'Arlevé)
Level: Hiker
Time: 5 hours 30 min
Elevation: descent 1,000 m, ascent 771 m, Descent 369 m
IGN 3531ET map or Pays du Mont-Blanc hiking map (A1 Rando Editions)
Access: Brévent cable car parking lot in Chamonix.

08 I Pont d'Arlevé

This is a hike in the valley of the Diosaz off the beaten track. With a start at the Brévent belvedere, where there is a beautiful view of the Mont-Blanc massif, the Bossons and Taconnaz glaciers and Chamonix.

At the ticket office, take a oneway ticket to Planpraz + Brévent and a return to Planpraz. Take the Planplaz gondola then the Planpraz Brévent cable car (2,525 m). Enjoy the view on arrival at the gazebo of the Mont-Blanc mountain range, its peaks and glaciers: Aiguilles de Chamonix, Aiguille du Midi, Mont-Blanc du Tacul, Mont-Maudit, Mont-Blanc, Dome du Goûter, the Bossons and Taconnaz glaciers. The view also extends to the Fiz massif. Viewpoint.

From the arrival station of the Brévent, cable car, on the right follow the direction to the Brévent pass. Along the way, keep your eyes skinned as you can see ibex and marmots. At the Col du Brévent (2,368 m), take the path on the left GR 5 towards the Col d'Anterne refuge.

A long journey down to the Pont d'Arlevé (1,597 m), which crosses the Diosaz. A Bucolic little trail and not often used through the flowers and streams stemming from Le Lac Cornu and Les Lacs Noirs. The main focus being the Fiz rocks and the Col d'Anterne refuge which will be difficult to reach there and back in a day. Half-way down between the pass and the bridge, you will pass the ruins of Arlevé cottages.

Have a Picnic at Arlevé bridge then go back along the same route, but the views are obviously different. In focus this time, the Charlanon peak and the top of Brévent.

After a good elevation climb (770 m), one returns to the Col du Brévent. From the pass, go back down towards Planpraz, again facing the Mont-Blanc.

Take the Planpraz gondola that takes you back to the Brévent car park in Chamonix.

Altitude: 2,317 m
Level: Hiker
Time: 3 hours
Elevation: 1,909 m to 2,310 m
IGN map 3630 OT or Pays du Mont-Blanc hiking map (A1 Rando Editions)
Access: From the Montenvers station car park in Chamonix.
Return to Aiguille du Midi cable car station in Chamonix.

09 I Grand Balcon Nord

A path that starts at the historical site of Montenvers and its splendid views on the Mer de Glace, the Drus and the Grandes Jorasses. A wonderful balcony crossing from Montenvers to Plan de l'Aiguille via the Signal de Forbes and its extraordinary panorama. Before your eyes is the great book of nature, between two exceptional sites, from the Mer de Glace to the Mont-Blanc.

At the Montenvers station, take a oneway ticket to Mer de Glace and a return from the middle station of the Aiguille du Midi cable car (Plan de l'Aiguille, the first section).

Take the little red trammel train which brings you to the foot of the Mer de Glace in 20 minutes. The site is very popular with tourists, so it is better to leave early to avoid the crowds and enjoy the points of interest before the hike.

From the Montenvers Grand Hotel, follow the direction of the Forbes Signal. Do not take the path specified « escarpé » (steep) that travels above the Chamonix valley, because as much as this trail is nice for people not suffering from vertigo, you miss the signal de Forbes view point.

The stroll begins with a winding climb up to the Signal of Forbes (2,198 m) marked by a multitude of cairns. The Signal of Forbes offers a 360° panoramic view opposite the Mer de Glace, the Drus and the Grandes Jorasses pool.

(After having your eyes full), you go downhill to the intersection with the « escarpé » trail coming directly from Montenvers.

The trail then travels in an obvious manner virtually on a balcony under the Aiguilles de Chamonix, facing the Aiguille du Midi and the Mont-Blanc, between lawns and boulders left behind by an ancient glacier.

It is recommended to picnic along the way before the Plan de l'Aiguille refuge. From the Plan de l'Aiguille refuge one dominates all the valley of Chamonix, facing the Brévent and the Aiguilles Rouges.

Before coming back down to Chamonix by using the first section of the Aiguille du Midi cable car from Plan de l'Aiguille, you can leave the path and get closer to pylons to the left, for the fantastic view over the Glacier des Bossons.

Once in Chamonix, you join the station of Montenvers where you left from in the morning being 10 minutes by foot, from the center.

The itinerary for the crossing of the Grand Balcon Nord is described in the guides the other way around. But then it is a real hikers'highway with a congested arrival at the Mer de Glace among a crowd of tourists. Thus, the direction proposed here makes more sense.

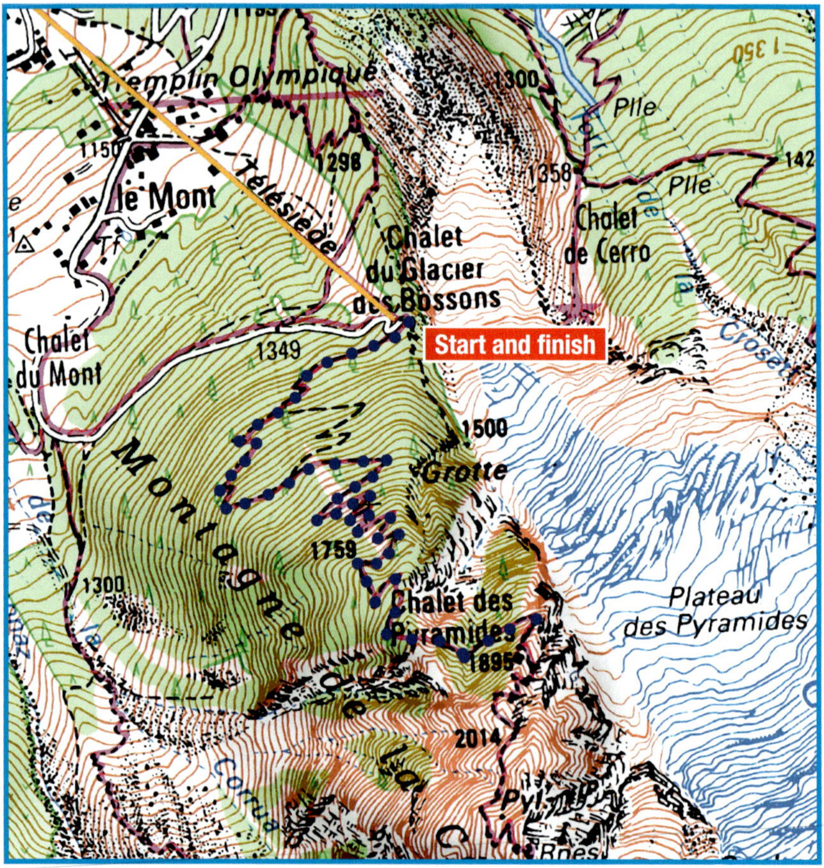

Altitude: 1,895 m
Level: Hiker
Time: Ascent 1 hour 30 min, Descent 1hour (Chalet des Pyramides, roundtrip with the Bossons chairlift)
Elevation: ascent 470 m, descent 470 m
IGN map 3630 OT or Pays de Mont-Blanc hiking map (A1 Rando Editions)
Access: Summit of the Bossons chairlift
Bossons chairlift car park, exit 205 N between Chamonix and Les Houches, then direction "Bossons glacier-Tremplin de saut".

10 | Chalet des Pyramides

This hike is a rather unrewarding steep climb through pine trees but which enables you to walk alongside the left bank of the Bossons glacier and gives you an exceptional view of its tip and the séracs of the Plateau des Pyramides.

At the Bossons car park, take the chairlift that takes you near the Bossons glacier (1,425 m). (You can also walk up to the Bossons glacier chalet in about 1 hour and 250 m elevation but it is of little interest).

The chairlift drops you at the Bossons glacier chalet from where you can enjoy the terrace, and the view of the tip of the glacier. An explanation in the form of a theme trail lined with panels tells the story of the glacier.

The chalet is the starting point for the hike up to the chalet des Pyramides. The trail climbs steadily, winding through the forest. Gaps in the wood allow regular views of the glacier. You reach the Chalet des Pyramides in about two hours, after a tedious climb.

There are few places for a picnic near the glacier in this unique setting that offers a breathtaking view of the glacier's sérac cascade. You can also take a snack at the Chalet des Pyramides.

The descent is via the same route. From the Bossons glacier chalet, you can take the chairlift down to the parking lot or by way of the trail named "Chemin des Monts", which is a small hamlet located above the Bossons and the ski slopes, allow 30 minutes. From the chalet des Pyramids, experienced hikers can continue towards La Jonction (2,589 m). The trail follows the Mountain de la Côte and takes you to the gates of the high mountains, with a magnificent view of the Bossons and Taconnaz glaciers situated on both sides. This route was taken by Jacques Balmat and Dr. Paccard during the first ascent of the Mont-Blanc in 1786. Allow 4 hours to reach the junction from the Bossons chairlift and 3 hours for the descent.

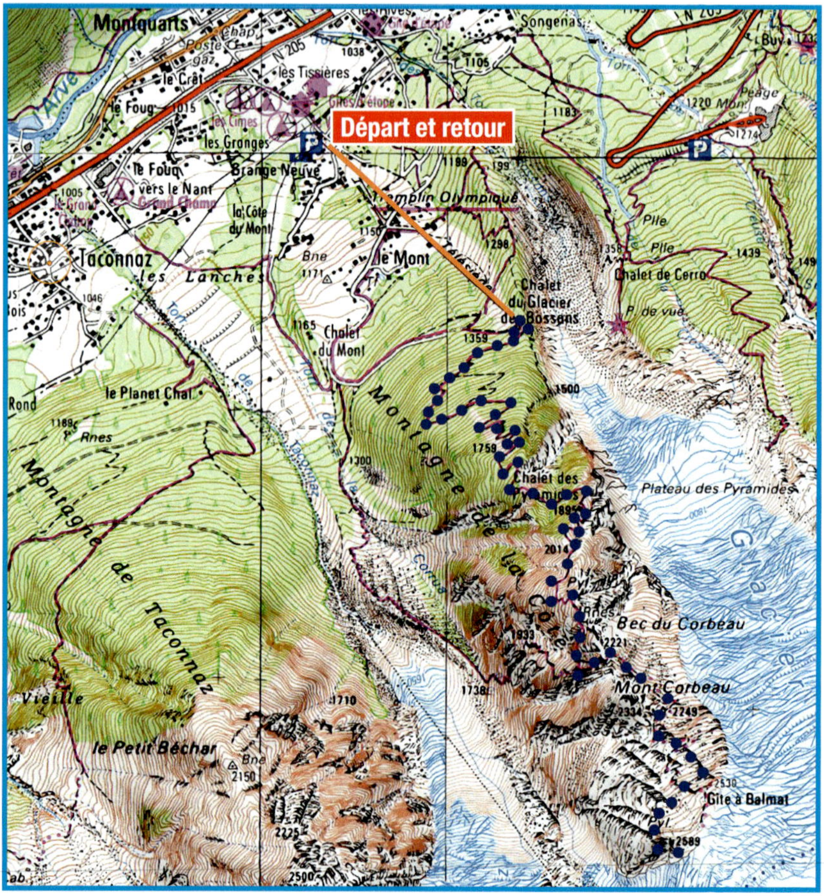

Altitude: 2,589 m
Level: Experienced hiker
Time: 3h45 up, 2h45 back (with Bossons chairlift round trip)
Elevation: 1,165 m up, 1,165 m down
Map: IGN 3630 OT
Access: Top of the Bossons chairlift (http://www.lavormaine.com). To reach the Bossons chairlift parking, exit on N205 between Chamonix and Les Houches, then head towards "Glacier des Bossons, Tremplin de Saut." Ideal good weather hike. Plan for a morning departure.

11 I La Jonction

This trail goes along the Montagne de la Côte and takes you up to the high mountain with a magnificent view over the Bossons and Taconnaz glaciers, located opposite each other. No other path gets this close to the summit of Mont Blanc. Jacques Balmat and doctor Michel Paccard took this itinerary during the first hike up to Mont Blanc in 1786.

Take the chairlift at Bossons. It should drop you off in 15 min at the Glacier des Bossons chalet (1,425 m). (You can also hike up to the Glacier des Bossons chalet – it takes about 1 hour with 250 m of elevation but it's not a particularly interesting hike).
The path winds up through the forest and regular clearings allow for views of the Taconnaz and Bossons glaciers. You'll reach the Pyramides lodge, clinging to the side of the mountain, in around 1h30 after a fairly fast, yet somewhat tedious ascent through the pine trees (see Hike 10).
Continue to follow the path above the lodge. The path winds like a snake over the Montagne de la Côte, between the right bank of the Taconnaz glacier and the left bank of the Bossons glacier.
After 2h30, you'll reach a view over 2 glaciers. A little further on you'll find a rougher, sports rate route, marked along the rock and occasionally equipped with a handrail and footboards.

At the end of this rocky ledge, you'll arrive at the Gîte à Balmat, granite blocks under which Balmat set up camp in his quest to reach Mont Blanc. The view is exceptional over all the Arve Valley, from Argentière all the way to Sallanches, the Aiguilles Rouges, the Brévent, the Fiz chain, the Aravis chain and the Houches plateau.
Soon after, you'll reach the Jonction, the historic summit of the Montagne de la Côte and the last point along this hiking trail. Picnic here – far from the rest of the world – at the heart of a spectacular show of glaciers, ridges, crevasses and peaks in front of 3 mountains: Mont Blanc du Tacul, Mont Maudit, and Mont Blanc, to the right of the Aiguille du Goûter and to the left of the Aiguille du Midi. Pay attention and you'll also notice the Grands Mulets refuge (3,151 m) in front of you, poised on a rocky island surrounded by ice. The descent heads back along the same trail. Allow for 1h45 to reach the Pyramides lodge and 1 hour more to get to Glacier chalet.

Altitude: 2,338 m
Level: Easy
Time: 2 hours
Elevatio: Ascent 362 m
IGN 3630 OT map or Pays du Mont-Blanc hiking map (A1 Rando Editions)
Access: Grand Montets cable car in Argentière.

12 I Viewpoint of the Argentière glacier

An easy route to a spectacular view over the sérac waterfalls of the Argentière glacier.

At the ticket office, take a return ticket to the intermediate station of La Croix-de-Lognan. Leaving the mid-point station Grands Montets (1,976 m), turn left onto the dirt road toward the Lognan refuge.
After about 15 minutes, you can see the Lognan refuge on left below the track. Ignore on your right the path going up which cuts through the mountain that you will take on the return leg. Keep to the track which soon brings you to a first view of the glacier.
Then follow the path overlooking the moraine until the higher Viewpoint (2,338 m) which is reached in under an hour. Impressive view of the sérac waterfalls and crevasses of the glacier below. After the higher Viewpoint, the trail goes down and begins on the left lateral moraine. Do not venture there, the route is for experienced hikers only, equipped for glacier hikes, who will join the Argentière refuge.

Turn around and go back down the trail on your left leading away from the glacier and which joins the dirt road taken in the morning, this leads to the intermediate station of the Grands Montets cable car. Before starting this walk, you can take the Grands Montets (preferably in the morning before the arrival of high clouds) leaving the station via Lognan. In this case, ask for a return ticket Grand-Montets.
The Grands Montets (3,295 m) are a beautiful gazebo with a viewpoint. View of the Argentière glacier, spectacular panorama with in the foreground the Drus, the Aiguille du Midi, the Mont-Blanc, the Dôme and the Aiguille du Goûter. On the other side of the valley, the Aiguilles Rouges.
You can also follow up this trail with hike N°11 (Chalets de la Pendant, Le Chapeau, Le Lavancher). In this case, do not take a return ticket to the intermediate station of Croix-de-Lognan in Argentière.

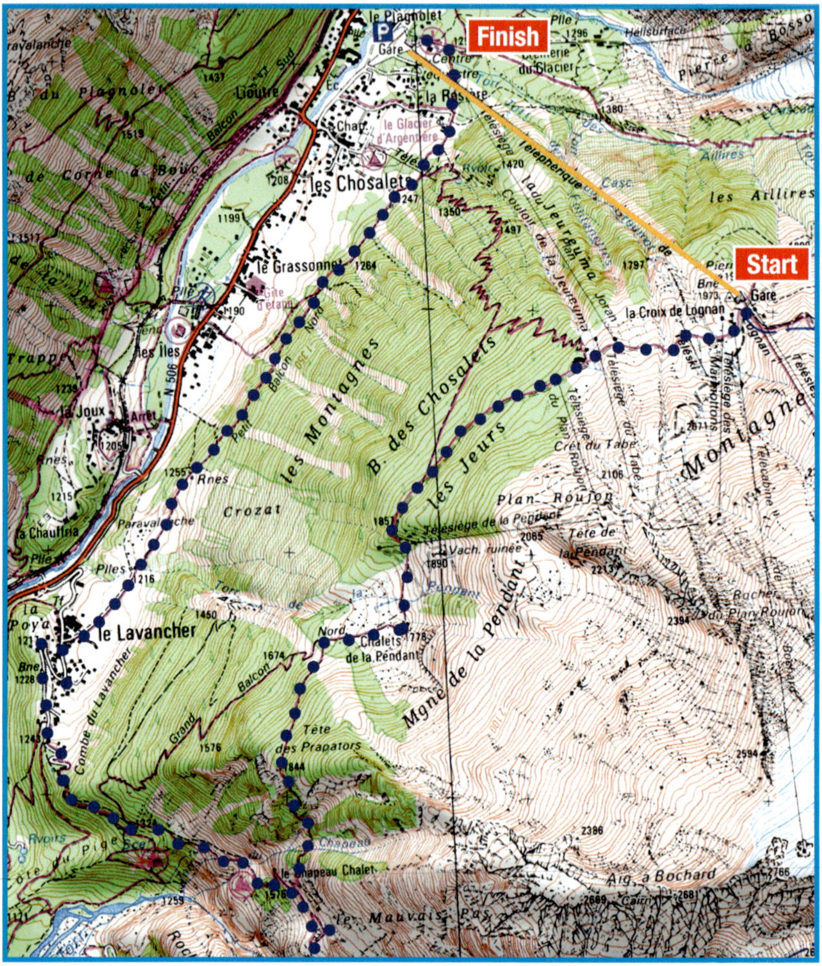

Altitude: 1,976 m (Lognan)
Level: Easy
Time: 3 hours
Elevation Descent 732 m
IGN 3630 OT map or Pays du Mont-Blanc hiking map (A1 Rando Editions)
Access: Grands Montets cable car in Argentière

13 I La Pendant, le Chapeau, le Lavancher chalets

An all downhill hike between pastures and larch forests with overviews on the Mer de Glace sector. Long ago, the Mer de Glace glacier came right up to the hamlet of Les Bois.

At the ticket office, take a one way ticket to the intermediary station of Croix de Lognan. When leaving the middle station of Grands-Montets (1,976 m), turn right onto the Grand Balcon Nord trail towards the la Pendant/le Lavancher chalets.

It is not unusual to see marmots at the beginning of the hike.

On your right, ignore the path going down towards the Chosalets.

The balcony trail crosses a larch forest then after crossing the stream, it joins the La Pendant pasture and its chalets (1,778 m).

After the chalets, leave the Grand Balcon Nord trail and take left towards the Têtes des Prapators (1,844 m) which is reached after passing through a thick forest.

Take the path that climbs to the Chapeau refuge by the Tête des Prapators.

From the lookout, the descent to the chalet is made through woodland. Views emerge and reveal the Mont-Blanc, the tip of the Mer de Glace glacier and in the foreground one can see Les Drus, in the background La Dent du Géant (Giant's tooth). One can easily observe the retreating glacier replaced by rock debris torn from the mountain.

Before joining the bar, La Buvette du Chapeau, one arrives at the crossroads leading to the Mauvais Pas, former lookout on the tip end of the Mer de Glace glacier before its retreat. This part is a round-trip of about an hour.

Back at the crossroads, you reach the bar, la Buvette du Chapeau (1,576 m) below.

One passes the lovely Chapeau waterfall with rock climbing cliffs at its feet.

Soon, one joins the Grand Balcon Nord trail that leads to the right. Carry on towards the village of Lavancher (1,243 m), a small and stylish village which has managed to keep its character and authenticity. In the village, turn right on Petit Balcon Nord to reach the parking of Grands Montets at Argentière, through meadows and forests,.The trail goes along the valley floor and on the left you leave the hamlets of La Joux, Les Iles, Le Grassonnet and Les Chosalets. You can also combine this hike with Hike N° 10 (Argentière glacier view). In this case, start by walking Hike N°10 and go on to do Hike N° 11.

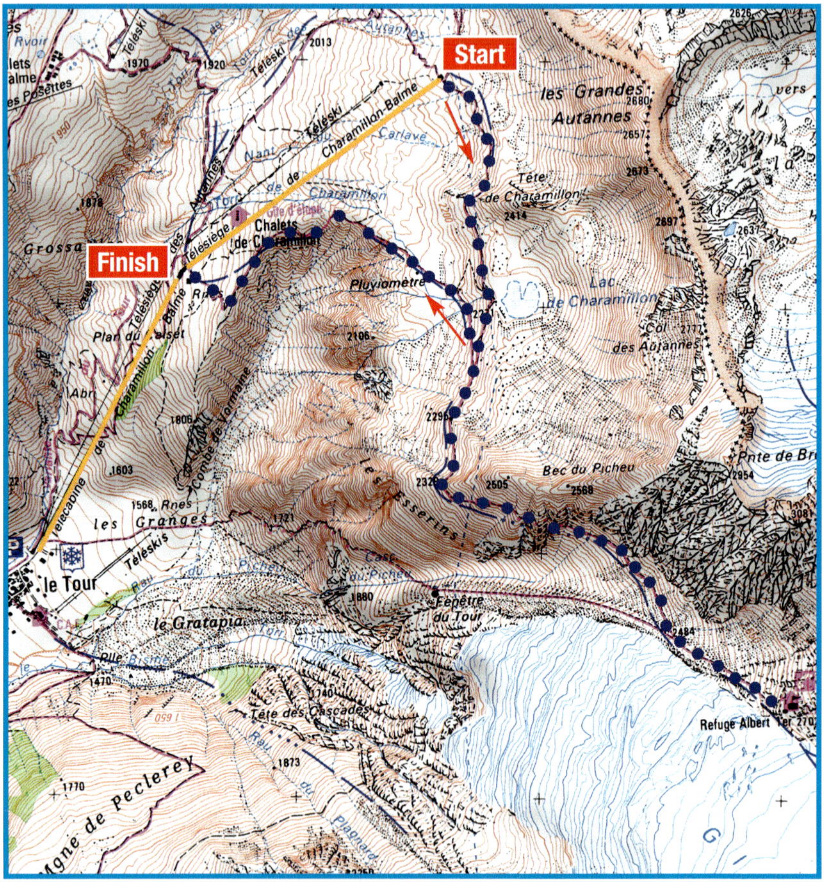

Altitude: 2,702 m
Level: Hiker
Time: Ascent 2 hours + descent 1 hour 30 min
Elevation: 2,185 m to 2,702 m
IGN map 3630 OT or Pays du Mont-Blanc hiking map (A1 Rando Editions)
Access: Charamillon gondola parking at the village of Tour
After Argentière (N 506) towards the Col des Montets, take a sharp right onto the small road in the direction of Le Tour
Albert 1er refuge kept from mid June to mid-September: 04 50 54 06 20

14 I Refuge Albert 1er

The Albert 1er refuge is one of the must-visit hikes of Chamonix. Along the way, one goes alongside the Tour glacier and its impressive crevasses. The refuge marks the gateway to the high mountain, with a magnificent view of the Aiguille du Chardonnet.

At the ticket office, take a one-way ticket Charamillon cable car + Autannes chairlift and return Charamillon cable car.
Upon arrival at the chairlift, take a right on the path leading to lake Charamillon and the Albert 1er refuge.
Once there, enjoy the view of the Mont-Blanc from a different angle.
After a half hour, ignore a path on the left, that goes up to the dried up lake of Charamillon. One quickly joins a crossroads, to the right of which is a path leading up to the middle station of Charamillon that you will follow on the return leg. Continue along the even trail, where the landscape unfolds bend after bend.
After about an hour, one can already see the Tour glacier, before reaching an area equipped with handrails, to negotiate a short steep passage.
After 1h30, you set foot on the moraine of the glacier at an intersection on the right of which is a path that climbs by the edge of the moraine from the village of the Tour. One dominates the glacier's séracs and crevasses which is very impressive. You can also see the refuge at the bottom of the ice plateau overhanging it.
Then begins the steep final climb (2,702 m) with the refuge in target that you reach by a rocky path in two hours. Behind the refuge, you have beautiful views, particularly on the Tour and Chardonnet peaks. After that is the sector for glacier hikes to nearby Switzerland or for mountaineers to the Peaks. You can picnic above the refuge on the edge of the glacier (bring warm clothes) in the company of yellow beaked jackdaws (large crows). You may be able to observe roped climbers in the middle of the vastness.
For the return leg, take the same route back. At the intersection of the Tour panel, do not take the path that goes down following the moraine of the glacier towards the Tour, but take the path on the right taken in the morning.
After an hour you reach the intersection crossed in the morning. This time, take the trail to the left that goes down through the Balme pastures and its herds of Herens cows towards the middle station of Charamillon. Ignore the path on the right taken in the morning, that goes back to the Autannes chairlift.
The route back offers views of the Emosson dam and the Aiguilles Rouges.

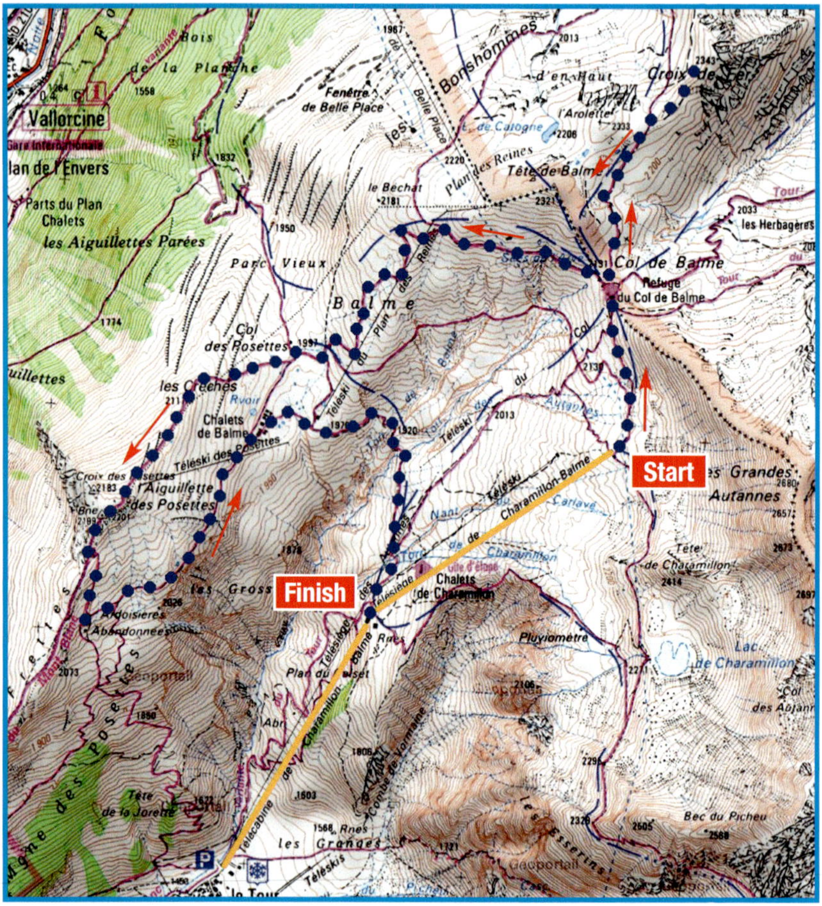

Altitude: 2,343 m
Level: Hiker
Time: 3 hours 30 min
Altitude: ascent 361 m, descent 635 m
IGN map 3630 OT
Access: Charamillon gondola parking at the village of Le Tour
After Argentière (N506) towards the Col des Montets, quickly take the small road to the right towards Le Tour.

15 I Col de Balme, Croix de Fer, Col des Posettes

This is a walk over the largest areas of pastures of the Chamonix valley. Rangeland edged courses leading to the Croix de Fer and the Aiguilles des Posettes that offer incomparable unobstructed 360° views over the valleys of Vallorcine, the Rhone and Chamonix but also a new outlook on the Mont-Blanc mountain range.

At the ticket office, take a one way ticket to the Charamillon gondola + Autannes Chairlift and return Charamillon gondola.
At the chairlift (2,186 m), turn left on the dirt road towards the Col de Balme (2,191 m). The Col de Balme marks the Franco-Swiss border.
One can already see the Balme refuge which is only a few minutes above the chairlift arrival. Enjoy the view of the Mont-Blanc from yet another angle.
Ignore the TMB on your right leading to the Forclaz Pass and on your left towards the Posettes pass, this trail you will follow later.
Head straight ahead beyond the Swiss border in the direction of the Croix de Fer.
One gets to a fork where on the left you ignore the path going down to the Catogne chalets visible below a steep incline, to follow on the right, a ridge that leads straight to the point of view of the Croix de Fer (2,343 m). Allow 30 to 45 minutes for a round trip to the Croix de Fer from the fork. From there, the view slips to the district of Valais, the Forclaz pass and the Rhone Valley.
Go back to the Col de Balme then follow the direction of Col des Posettes (1,997m) where you can picnic.
After climbing the ridge between the valley of Chamonix and Vallorcine valley, you reach the Aiguilles des Posettes (2,201 m) which offers an overview of 360°. The view flies over the Mont-Blanc range from the glaciers of Trient, the Tour and Argentière then the Aiguilles Rouges, as far as the Aiguille du Goûter but also up to Mont Buet and the Emosson dam.
For the return, one has several possibilities. The nicest and the shortest is the one that takes you back to the middle station of Charamillon, via the Chalets de Balme and down through the pasture of Balme and its herds of Hérens cows. To do this, follow the direction of the Chalets de Balme ignoring the TMB path towards Tré-le-Champ on your right.
From the Chalets de Balme, leave the path which goes down to the Tour and turn left 180° towards the middle station of Charamillon.

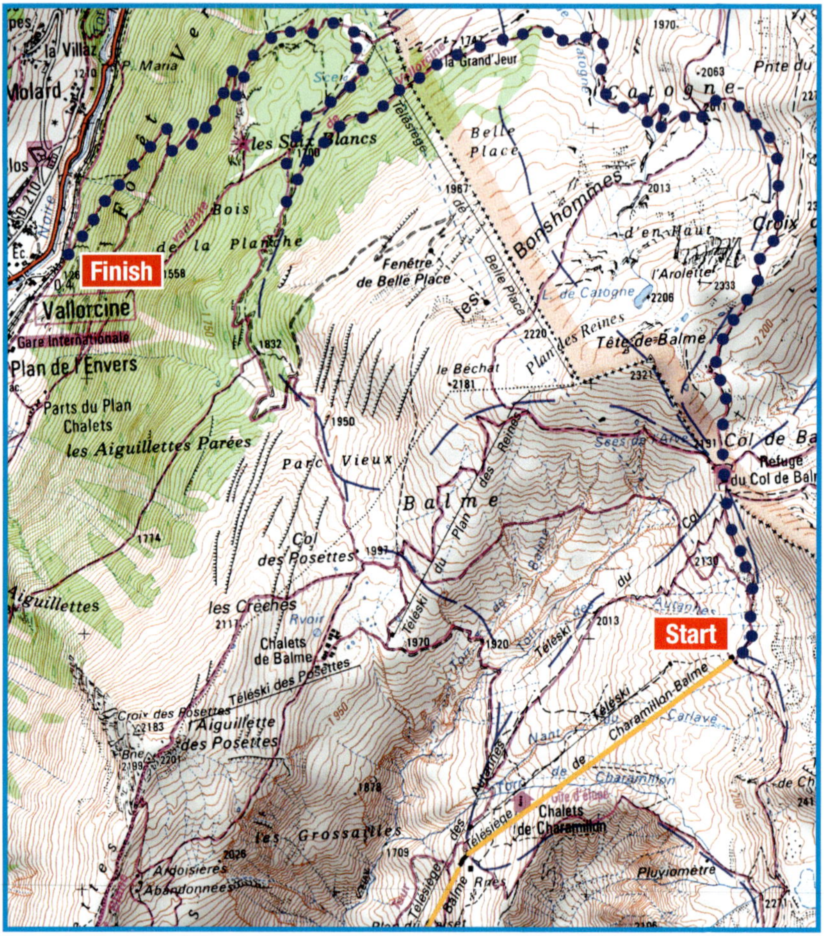

Altitude: 2,343 m
Level: Hiker
Time: 3 hours
Elevation gain: Ascent 157 m, Descent 1,079 m
IGN map 3630 OT or Pays du Mont-Blanc hiking map (A1 Rando Editions)
Access: Charamillon gondola at the village of Tour; Bus n°1 – Chamonix-Le Tour
Return by train Vallorcine-Chamonix.

16 I Col de Balme, Croix de Fer, Vallorcine or le Buet

This is a stroll through the Charamillon and Balme pastures still hosting the Héren cows in summer. A new viewpoint on the Mont-Blanc mountain range. A course on the mountain ridge towards the Iron Cross which offers an unobstructed view of the Rhone and Vallorcine valleys. And finally, the descent towards the villages of Vallorcine or Le Buet with a view of the pretty village of Châtelard located below the Emosson dam.

At the ticket office, take a one way ticket to the Charamillon gondola + Autannes chairlift. At the chairlift (2,186 m), turn left on the dirt road towards the Col de Balme (2,191 m). The Col de Balme marks the Franco-Swiss border.
One can already see the the refuge of Balme which is only a few minutes over the chairlift. Enjoy the view of the Mont-Blanc from another angle.
Leave the TMB on your right leading to the Forclaz pass and on your left towards the Posettes pass.
Head straight ahead beyond the Swiss border in the direction of the Iron Cross. You arrive at a fork where on the left you ignore the path going down to the Catogne chalets visible below, but take the ridge path on your right leading to the Iron Cross viewpoint (2,343 m). Allow 30 to 45 minutes for a round trip to the Iron Cross from the fork. From there, the vista lies on the District of Valais, the Forclaz pass and the Rhone Valley.

Back at the fork, take the path going under the Iron Cross towards the Catogne chalets. Once you arrive at an intersection, continue straight on (ignoring on the right the Trient direction and on the left up towards the Balme/Posettes passes).
Cross the Balme pasture with its herds of Hérens cows. You continue downhill and reach the start of the Tête de Balme chairlift from where one has a nice view of the village of Châtelard just below the Emosson dam. You can picnic here.
Shortly after, leave the path that goes back to the Posettes pass and turn right on a path at 180° which goes down towards Vallorcine. You reach a fork where the path splits into two branches, one on the right that joins the resort of Vallorcine through a pine forest and the other on the left leading to the Buet. If you choose Vallorcine, you can then reach the train station of Buet by the stagecoach path.
To return to Chamonix, take the Mont-Blanc-Express train, Martigny-Saint-Gervais line, either from Vallorcine station, or from Buet station.

Altitude: 1,969 m (Prarion) and 2,115 m (Mont-Lachat)
Level: Hiker
Time: 3 hours 30 min (or 3 hours if one takes the Mont-Blanc Tramway from the Voza pass at Bellevue)
Elevation: 1,860 m to 2,115 m (Climb up 116 + 133 + 329 m + 316 + 329 m downhill)
IGN 3531ET or Pays du Mont-Blanc hiking map (A1 Rando Editions)
Access: Summit of the Les Houches-Prarion gondola.
Parking Prarion-Les Houches cable car found at the far end of the borough of Les Houches, in the direction of Les Chavants.

17 I Le Prarion and Mont-Lachat

A relaxing walk to discover amazing views and avoid large differences in altitude.

Take a round trip ski lift ticket (one way: Prarion; return to Bellevue).
Once you arrive at the top, the view of the Chamonix valley and the Mont-Blanc mountain range is beautiful. You can see the trace of the route at the top of the Mont-Blanc by the normal route which starts from the refuge of the Goûter.
Take the path on the right called the path of the "Tête du Prarion" that goes up the ridge through a sparse forest. It takes you up in 30 minutes to an exceptional view with a 360 ° panorama described as the "most beautiful overview in Europe". Viewpoint, views of the Mont-Blanc and Aravis massif, the Fiz limestone cliffs, the valley of the Arve, the Contamines-Monjoie valley, etc.

Go back on your steps by the same path to the Prarion Hotel-Cottages (15 minutes).
The hotel has a terrace facing the Mont-Blanc, where you can have lunch, there are also nice deckchairs for a coffee or drink.
Then follow the path to the pasture of La Charme leading down (20 minutes) among the rhododendrons and heather to the farm (goat cheese). At La Charme (1,799 m), head to the Voza pass (20 minutes), the path crosses the forest and then goes down a rocky path to the Voza pass (1,653 m).
At the Voza pass, you can walk along the right of the railway track after crossing it, to get to Bellevue (35 minutes) or take the Mont-Blanc Tramway to get to a station. If time allows, I recommend the latter solution because the climb to Bellevue along the railroad is not of much interest.
Once at Bellevue, take the path behind the terrace of the cable car snack bar. The over-hanging path on the Chamonix valley offers a permanent view of the Aiguille du Midi and the Aiguilles de Chamonix. It takes you within an hour to the summit of Mont-Lachat where the dominant view extends to 360°. 200 m before the Mont-Lachat pass and its derelict station, turn right to reach a grassy plateau. There is a superb view on the Bionnassay glacier and its valley.
Return via the same pathway (30 minutes). Take the Bellevue gondola up to Les Houches. You can reach Les Houches Prarion cable car parking lot in 10 minutes by following the road on the left. If you wish to go back down to Les Houches from Bellevue by the Grand-Bois path in the forest, add one hour.

Valley of Vallorcine

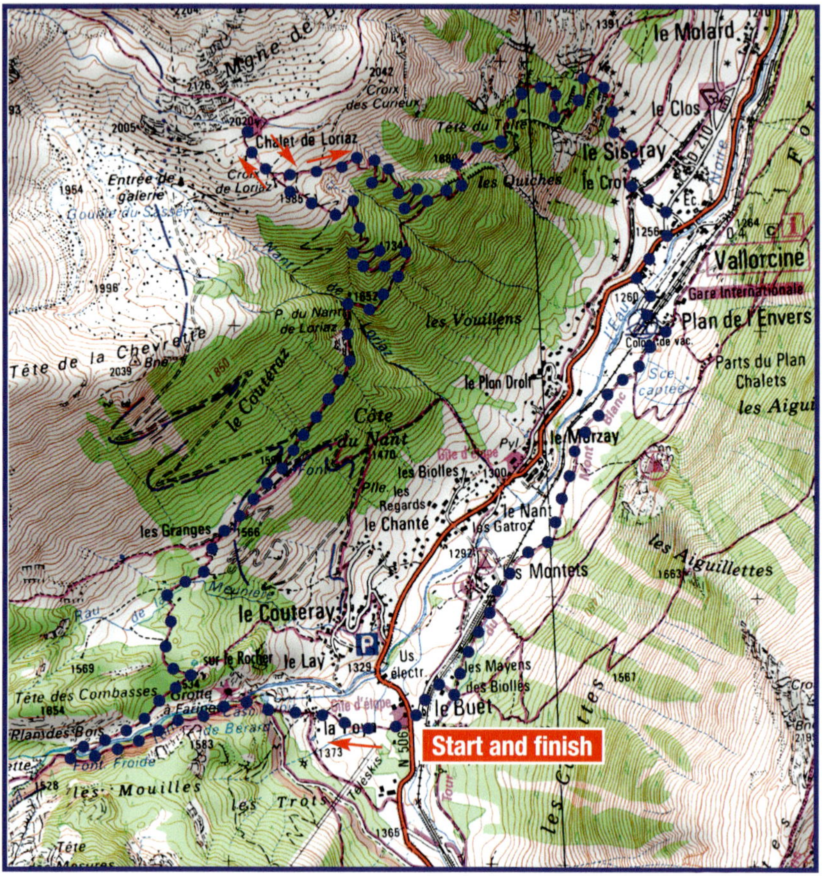

Altitude: 2,020 m
Level: Hiker
Time: Ascent 2 hours 30 min + Descent 1 hour 30 min
Elevation: 1,340 m to 2,020 m
IGN map 3630 OT or Pays du Mont-Blanc hiking map (A1 Rando Editions)
Access: Parking at Le Buet train station
After Argentière and the Col des Montets towards Vallorcine (N 506)
SNCF Line Saint-Gervais-Martigny, Le Buet station
Refuge kept from mid June to mid-September: 04 50 18 04 91

18 I Refuge de Loriaz

A walk in a loop starting from the Vallorcine valley to the alpine chalet refuge located in the heart of the Aiguilles Rouges from which one enjoys an exceptional view of the Mont-Blanc massif.

Just half a day is enough to do the roundtrip but a whole day allows you to enjoy the mountain pastures and why not have lunch at the refuge which is made up of "stables" built against each other (50 beds in three dormitories).
For experienced hikers, extension at the Col de la Terrasse (2,648 m) in 1h45 (way up only), Dinosaur traces by the Col de la Terrasse in 2h30 (one way only) or to Emosson lake by the Passet pass (balcony path equipped with handrails) in 1h30 (one way only).
There are several paths leading to the refuge. I suggest the loop from the Buet parking, return via Vallorcine (preferably to be carried out this way around).
Take the signposted trail "Refuge de la Pierre à Bérard" across the parking lot of Buet. The trail crosses the chalets of la Poya and then climbs into the forest.
Within 15 min, refreshment bar of the Eau de Bérard cascade. Follow the stream on its right bank to an intersection allowing you to cross the stream (one leaves the path of La Pierre à Bérard refuge) towards "Tré-les-Eaux" then follow "Les Granges". At Les Granges, (restored pasture houses), one must be alert, take if need be, the trail that progresses above the houses. The way to Loriaz is not indicated. Take the opposite direction at Tré-les-Eaux (right facing the mountain). The path then leads to a dirt road for about 200 m and then progresses on the edge of a forest (the way to Loriaz is now well indicated). One crosses the river of Le Nant de Loriaz. Climbing up through the pine trees, you see breathtaking views of the Grands, Tour, and Argentière glaciers, the Drus and the Aiguilles Rouges.
When you exit the forest floor, you get to the pasture where the Hérens cow bells herald the refuge. On the left, you will see a metal cross placed on a boulder.
The return can be done by Vallorcine. Retrace your steps, then follow the direction of Vallorcine at the junction Vallorcine/Le Buet. It's a long way down through the forest with beautiful apertures on the valley; allow a good hour to reach Vallorcine. At the locality named "Le Crot" you can take the road to join Vallorcine train station, then cross the railway tracks and take the stagecoach trail to get to the Buet parking lot. (Allow half an hour between Vallorcine and Buet stations).

Valley of Vallorcine

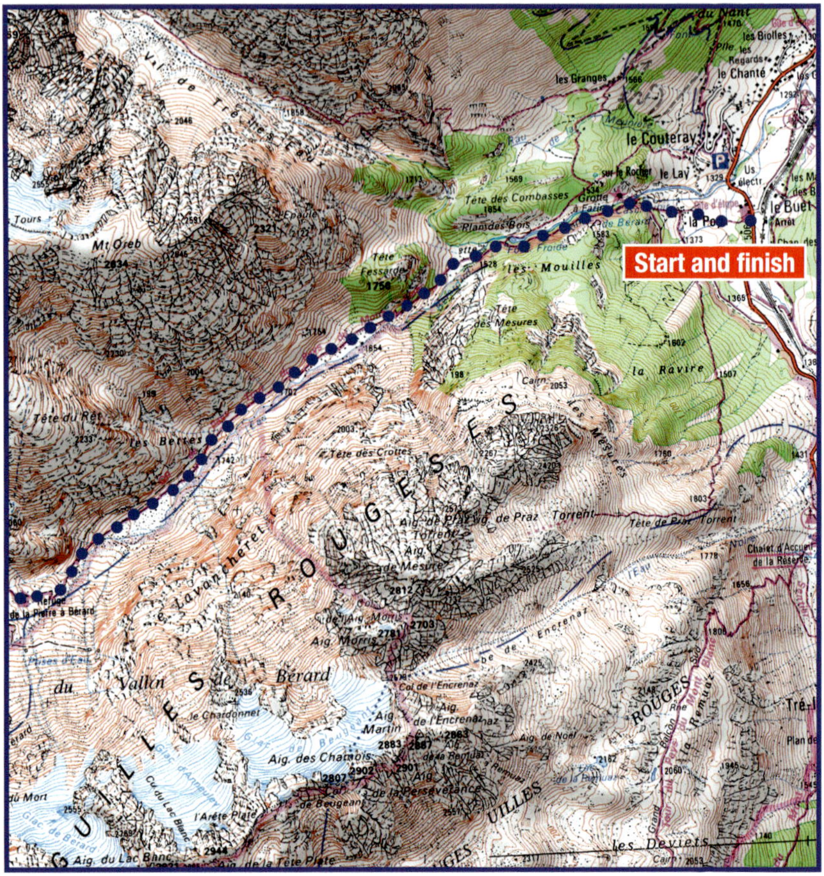

Altitude: 1,924 m
Level: Hiker
Time: Ascent 2 hours + Descent 1 hour 40 min
Elevation: 1,340 m to 1,924 m
IGN map 3630 OT or Pays du Mont-Blanc hiking map (A1 Rando Editions)
Access: Parking at Buet station
After the Argentière pass and Col des Montets towards Vallorcine (N 506)
SNCF Line Saint-Gervais-Martigny, Le Buet station
Refuge kept from mid June to mid-September: 04 50 54 62 08

19 I Refuge de la Pierre à Bérard

A round trip walk starting from the valley of Vallorcine to the alpine chalets refuge located in the heart of the Aiguilles Rouges from which one enjoys an exceptional view of the Mont-Blanc mountain range.

Half a day is enough for a round trip but a day is nice to enjoy the torrent on days when the sun is shining and snowfields can sometimes be seen above the refuge. (EDF warning sign risk of rapidly rising waters). Extension to the Bérard pass in 1h45 (climb only) or to the Salenton pass in 2 hours (climb only).

Blueberry picking on the way in season. Ibex and marmots if you're lucky. Well signposted path to follow starting opposite Le Buet parking lot.

The trail goes through the Poya village chalets and then climbs into the forest.

In 15 minutes, bar of the Eau de Bérard cascade. Continue along the right bank of the torrent (thus left of the torrent).

About 1,650 m, end of the forest floor. You advance into the valley of Bérard which later divides into two branches, take the one on the right to go up and back down by the one which follows the river closely.

The valley is dominated by the Buet foothills on the right and to the left by Les Aiguilles Rouges. In the distance one can see the refuge standing against its big stone block, once used as a landmark for shepherds to lead the flocks to pasture. The glaciers that were once much bigger, dominate the site.

For those who wish to climb Mont-Buet (3,096 m) the next day (about 3 hours up and 2 hours downhill), one can sleep at the refuge, (40 beds). Comfort: omelets, crusted Bérard, mountain plate, gratin of Crozet, tartiflettes, blueberry tarts, etc.

Valley of Vallorcine

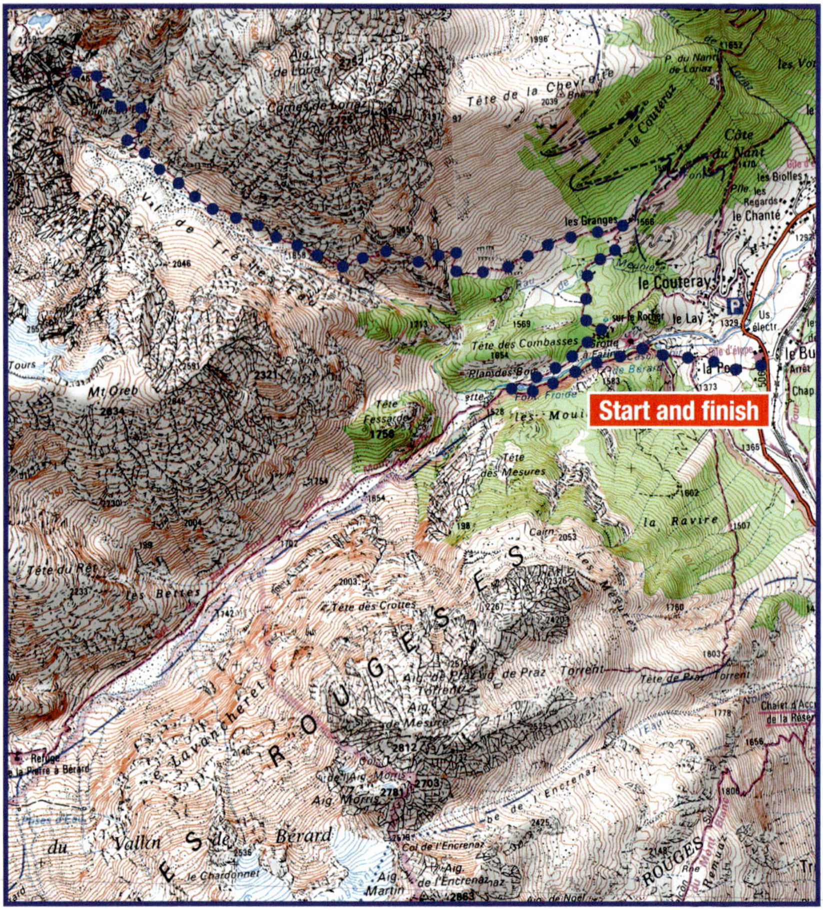

Altitude: 2,000 m
Level: Hiker
Time: 5 hours roundtrip the valley bottom (place called La Gouille du Bouc)
Elevation: from 1,340 m to 2,000 m
Map: IGN 3630 OT or Pays du Mont Blanc hiking map (A1, Rando edition)
Access: parking lot at Le Buet station, after Argentière and the Col des Montets when you're headed towards Vallorcine (N 506). SNCF line Saint-Gervais-Martigny, Le Buet station.

20 I Tré-les-Eaux Valley

Circular hike in a wild little valley. This route is rarely taken from the start of the Vallorcine valley, yet offers superb views over the Argentière and Tour glaciers.

Starting from the Buet parking lot and take the route marked "refuge de la Pierre à Bérard."
The trail passes by the Poya chalets and then climbs up towards the forest. After 15 min, take in the refreshing Eau de Bérard waterfall. Continue along the right bank of the water, and then cross at the first bridge over the stream (thereby leaving the Pierre à Bérard pathway and heading towards "Tré les Eaux" and "Les Granges"). Continue until you reach the point called "Sur le rocher" (1,539m, with small houses).
Just beyond "Sur le Rocher," you'll be confronted with two possibilities to reach the Tré-les-Eaux valley:
First, you can choose to take a trail allowing you to cross the rocky outcrop. It's a difficult and physically demanding passage that takes about 30 min.
Or, you can go around the rocky outcrop (towards Loriaz and then towards Tré-les-Eaux at the Granges fork).
If you choose to take the trail (and I suggest you only do so if the weather is nice), you'll cross over a flowery meadow and then head up along the left bank of a stream through a maze of chaotic stone blocks and wild strawberries and blueberries.
At the end of this difficult climb, you'll meet back up with the pathway that turns around the rocky outcrop.
Next you'll begin a 30-minute trip to the bottom of the La Gouille au Bouc valley, a wide wet valley at the foot of the Buet Mountain. The path snakes through a corridor full of rocks and thick pines. Nature in its purest state. The landscape is bare as you head to the bottom of the valley– thanks to the mountain sheep. Stop for a picnic in this area, far from the rest of the world, and take a break or continue on for another 45 min towards the Col des Corbeaux pass if you want to go a bit further up in elevation. It's quite worth it for the magnificent view over the Aiguille Verte, the Aiguille du Chardonnet, and the Argentière glacier.
The way back goes along the same route but in the opposite direction, with constant views over the Tour and Argentière glacial basins.
At the fork between the road and the bypass of the rocky ridge, head towards "Les Granges." Be careful after that– the trail no longer heads through scree on its way to Granges (via the old pathway now blocked by a cross on the rock to the left) but plunges to the right through the forest and towards the river on its way to Granges and "Sous Le Rocher."

Valley of Vallorcine

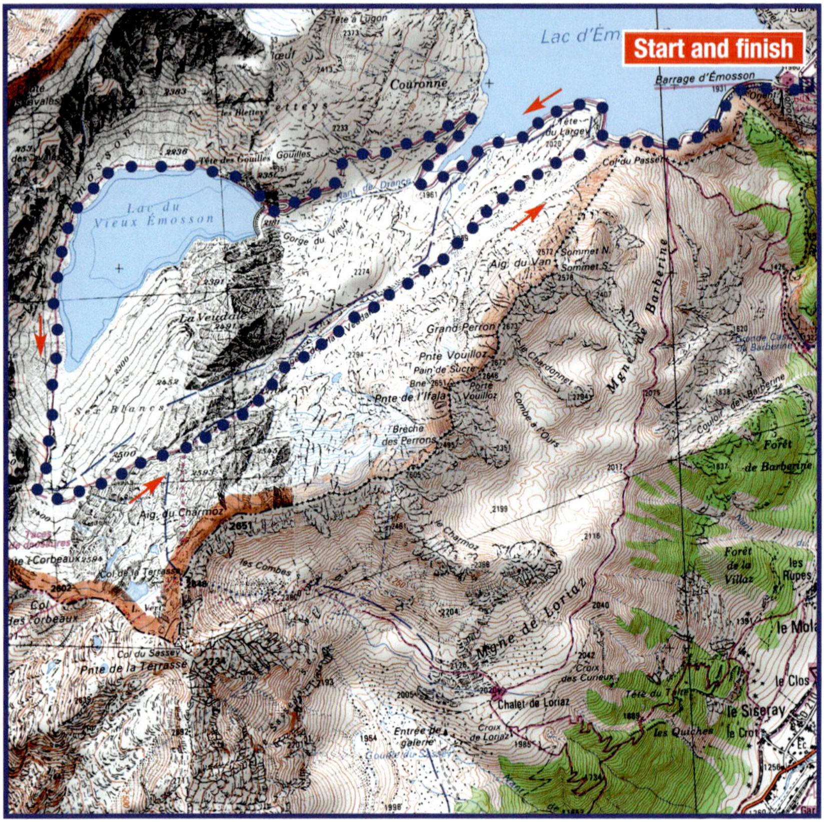

Altitude: 2,400 m (Dinosaur Tracks)
Level: Hiker
Time: 5 hours
Elevation: 1,960 m to 2,500 m
IGN 3630 OT map or the Pays du Mont-Blanc hiking map (A1 Rando Editions)
Access: Lake Emosson dam parking
After Argentière and the Col des Montets towards Vallorcine (N 506), cross the Swiss border. Shortly after the border (2 km), go left onto the small road towards Finhaut that winds up and ends at the Emosson dam.
Guided tours of the dam from mid-July to mid-August every day except Sunday at 11:30 am and 3 pm.

21 I Dinosaur Tracks

A geological hike of the region in nature's outstanding beauty. 250 million years ago, a herd of dinosaurs left their footprints on the site. Panoramic view of the Mont-Blanc and the Swiss Alps from the Emosson dam..

The Emosson dam is located at the Gueulaz pass, hike starting point. Enjoy the panoramic view of the Mont-Blanc and the Swiss Alps on one side and the lake's blue water and the impressive top of the dam on the other (height 180 m and 554 m length). Go down towards the dam. The route uses the paved road that crosses the dam and runs along the lake's edge to the left, towards the old Emosson lake.

One walks alongside old Emosson lake by the right then the trail takes you uphill to the site of the Dinosaur tracks (2,400 m). More than 800 footprints dating back 250 million years were discovered on the most famous site in Europe.

Late July/ early August, a geologist from the Natural History Museum of Geneva gives explanations on the site's tracks, every day from 11 am to 4 pm, weather permitting. For the return, one last climb takes you along a path on your left to the Col Suspendu (overlying pass, 2,500 m) where snowfields may remain.

The long descent is made along the Veulade coomb and its stream.

Experienced hikers who wish to extend the hike can make a round-trip detour (1h30) to the Col de la Terrasse (2,645 m), before going down. From the dinosaur tracks, take the path on the right towards the Col de la Terrasse trudging through a moonscape dotted with many small lakes. Conspicuous cairns guide you to the pass which offers stunning views of the Mont-Blanc massif and the trail below that climbs steeply through stone scree to the refuge of the Loriaz chalets. Retrace your steps.

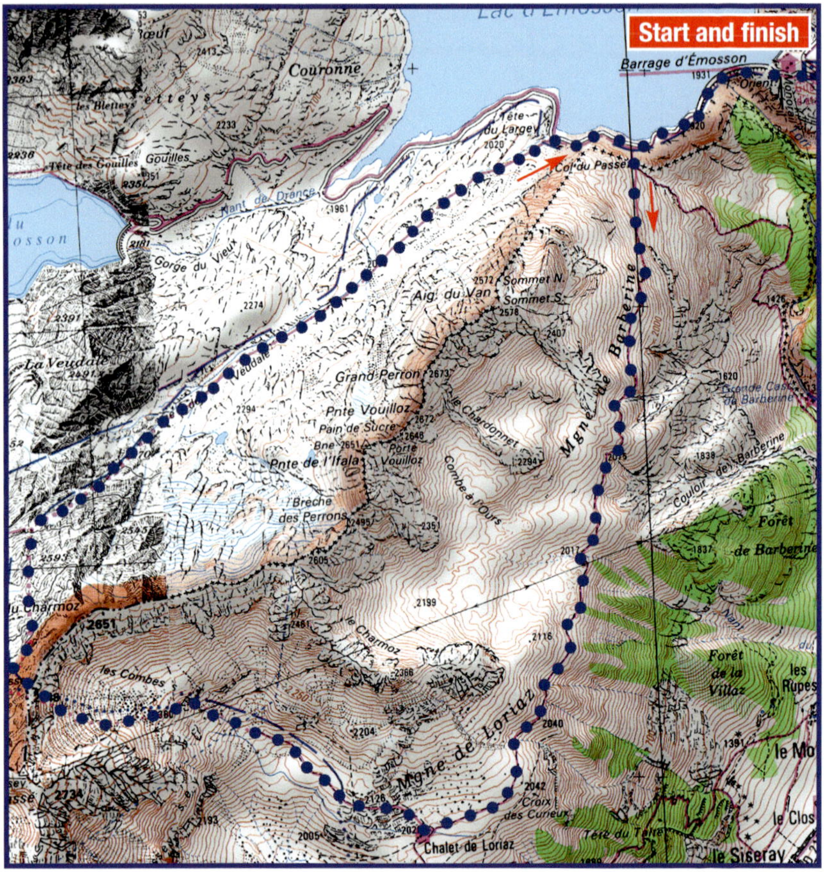

Altitude: 2,645 m
Level: Experienced Hiker
Time: 6 hours (Loriaz 1 hour 30 min + Col de la Terrasse 1 hour 45 min; Descent 2 hours 30 min)
Elevation: 1,960 m to 2,645 m
IGN map 3630 OT or the Pays du Mont-Blanc hiking map (A1 Rando Editions)
Access: Lake Emosson dam parking
After Argentière and the Col des Montets towards Vallorcine (N 506), cross the Swiss border. Shortly after the border (2 km), go left onto the small road towards Finhaut that winds up and ends at the Emosson dam.

22 I Refuge de Loriaz and Col de la Terrasse

A hike in a loop straddling Switzerland and France starting from Lake Emosson dam. Going through the alpine refuge chalets of Loriaz in the heart of the Aiguilles Rouges from which one enjoys an exceptional view of the Mont-Blanc mountain range. The satisfaction of having conquered the climb to the Terrasse pass where the view is stunning. The downhill country hike through the narrow valley of Veudale.

The Emosson dam is located at the Gueulaz pass, starting point for the hike. Enjoy the panoramic view of the Mont-Blanc and the Swiss Alps on one side and on the other of the lake's blue water and the impressive top of the dam (height 180 m and length 554 m).
Go down towards the dam. The itinerary follows the beginning of the paved road that crosses the dam's wall. Take the path to the left signed posted Col du Passet/Barberine /refuge de la Loriaz.

Quickly leave the hamlet of Barberine's path, take a left and continue towards La Loriaz. Handrail paths help to assist crossing the avalanche passages. Then the trail progresses easily along a balcony crossing the Barberine Mountain then that of Loriaz. You reach the pasture where the Hérens cow bells herald the refuge.
Have a rest at the chalets of Loriaz (2,020 m) before tackling the steep climb to the Col de la Terrasse, which winds through the rubble of the stony Ravin des Combes. Ibex along the way.
You can picnic at the pass, from where the view is stunning (when it is not in the clouds!)
At the Col de la Terrasse (2,645 m), leave the trail to the left, which heads toward the Col des Corbeaux and follow ahead, slightly to the right of conspicuous cairns that guide you to the Col Suspendu (2,500 m). The trail passes through a lunar landscape dotted with numerous small lakes. At the Col Suspendu, snowfields may remain.
The long downhill hike is made along the Veulade coombe and its stream.
The hike can be done the other way around to avoid the climb to the Terrasse pass and to take the dizzying downhill trail from the pass towards the chalets of the Loriaz. However, the hike as proposed, allows one to have permanent vues on the Mont-Blanc and its glaciers (Trient, Tour and Argentière) via the balcony path of the Barberine Mountain in the direction Emosson dam-Loriaz.

Valley of Vallorcine

Altitude: 2,665 m
Level: Experienced Hiker
Time: Ascent 3 hours 30 min + Descent 3 hours
Elevation: 1,526 m to 2,665 m
IGN map 3630 OT or the Pays du Mont-Blanc hiking map (A1 Rando Editions)
Access: Parking Forclaz pass
After Argentière and the col des Montets towards Vallorcine (N 506), cross the Swiss border then go back up to the pass.

23 I Fenêtre de l'Arpette

A physically demanding hike in steep terrain on a rocky trail for a climb up to the Col de l'Arpette. Lovely views of the Trient glacier over much of the trail, which runs along the tip of the glacier.

You will gain to do this hike on a day when it is not too hot and to leave around 9:00 am from the pass to picnic at the Arpette window before going down.
The path is well signposted, starting from the Forclaz pass on the right when you come from Chamonix.

From the pass to the Glacier's chalet-bar (50 minutes), the trail is flat and runs along the Bisse du Trient (small artificial canal) built in 1895, overlooking the village of Trient.
You arrive just before the Glacier chalet at a fork on the right towards the Col de Balme. Go straight ahead and do not cross the wooden bridge that crosses the stream (stay on the right bank of the stream); however, there is a beautiful view of the glacier from this footbridge. After the Glacier chalet, the trail runs in the middle of a thin forest of larch trees.
After walking 1h30 one arrives at the chalets of Vésevey (2,096 m), starting point of the steep climb (2 hours) in the middle of fallen rocks. On the way down you cross many hikers because Champex-Fenêtre de l'Arpette-Trient is a TMB Alpine version. During the climb, if you turn around there is a beautiful clear view of the Emosson dam. The slope becomes steeper, the vegetation disappears.
The arrival at the "Window", a narrow passage from one slope to the next, hence its name, is rather disappointing view wise from the Swiss side! (It is up to you to discover what lies behind the Arpette window, that's the aim!).
Time is not necessarily gained going downhill compared to going uphill because one must be cautious on the steep and stony slopes.
For those who do not feel able to go up to the Fenêtre de l'Arpette, the walk along the Trient glacier is sufficient unto itself, one can stop uphill between the Vésevey chalets and the Fenêtre de l'Arpette when you see the Emosson dam behind you in the distance. The more adventurous, can say "I made the Arpette!"
2h30 from the Fenêtre de l'Arpette to Champex.
See the variant loop of two days with a night at Champex before the return to Forclaz pass by Bovine (Hike N° 24).

Valley of Vallorcine

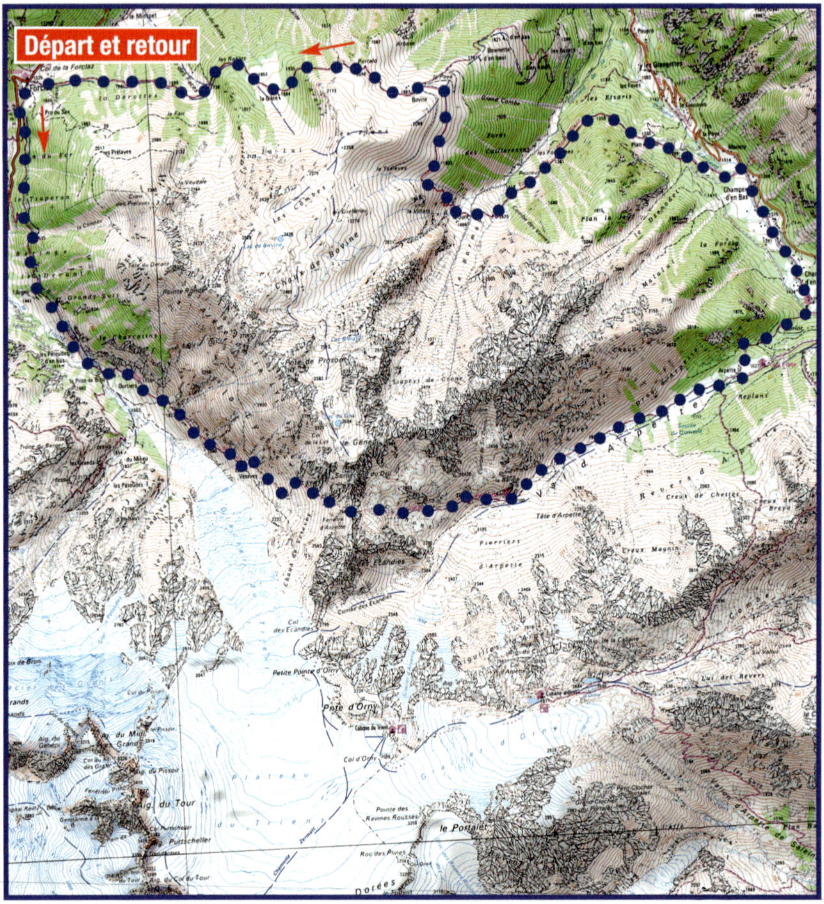

Altitude: 2,665 m
Level: Experienced Hiker
Schedule: 2 days, night in Champex in Switzerland (d1: 6 hours, d2: 5 hours 30 min)
Elevation gain: day 1: 1,139 m, day 2: 589 m
IGN map 3630 OT or Pays du Mont-Blanc hiking map (A1 Rando Editions)
Access: Col de La Forclaz parking
After Argentière and the Col des Montets towards Vallorcine (N 506), cross the Swiss border and then go up to the pass.

24 I Fenêtre de l'Arpette to Champex, Champex to Col de la Forclaz via Bovine

This two-day hike with a night in Champex in Switzerland starts from the Forclaz pass. The first day, you reach Champex by taking the same itinerary as hike N° 21 via the Fenêtre de l'Arpette. The return is done by following the Tour du Mont-Blanc itinerary via the Bovine alpine pastures. After the first day of hiking among the boulders, the second day is refreshing and rural between larch forests and alpine pastures.

For the first part of this hike, see hike N° 21 which allows access to the Fenêtre de l'Arpette in 3h30. One can picnic at the Fenêtre de l'Arpette before starting the long journey down to Champex which takes 2h30.

From the pass, the trail swings towards the valley of Arpette on a very steep slope through fallen rocks. The rocky trail continues much of the way down and runs alongside the river Arpette. At about 1,700 m one reaches the charming Arpette valley with its herds of Hérens cows. A wide gravel path leads to the Arpette hotel-restaurant (1,630 m). The trail continues to Champex-Lac through the undergrowth and along the Bisse (reach). You pass near the start of the Breya chairlift before gaining Champex-Lac (1,460 m) to spend the night (accommodation to be booked in advance).

Champex-Lac is a quiet resort in the enchanting site of the alpine lake of Champex and a major stage in the Tour du Mont-Blanc.

The second day, join the TMB and its well-marked route to the hamlet of Champex-d'En-Haut (1,434 m). Continue along the stream towards the village of Champex-d'En-Bas (1,359 m). After crossing the stream, the trail soon joins the pasture of Plan-de-l'Au (1,330 m). Allow about 1h15 from Champex-Lac. The first path goes gently sloping to the chalet de la Jure, then continues with a steep winding path. You reach the Bovine pastures then the chalets (1,975 m) in 2h30 from the Plan-de-l'Au. One can picnic at Bovine where there is a panoramic vue on Martigny, the Swiss Valais and the Rhone Valley.

It will take another 1h30 to reach the Col de La Forclaz (1,526 m). From Bovine, a final short climb to the Col de Portalo, highlight of the second day (2,049 m), then you tackle the descent into the forest via the chalet de La Giète (1,884 m) and its large clearing.

Valley of Bionnassay

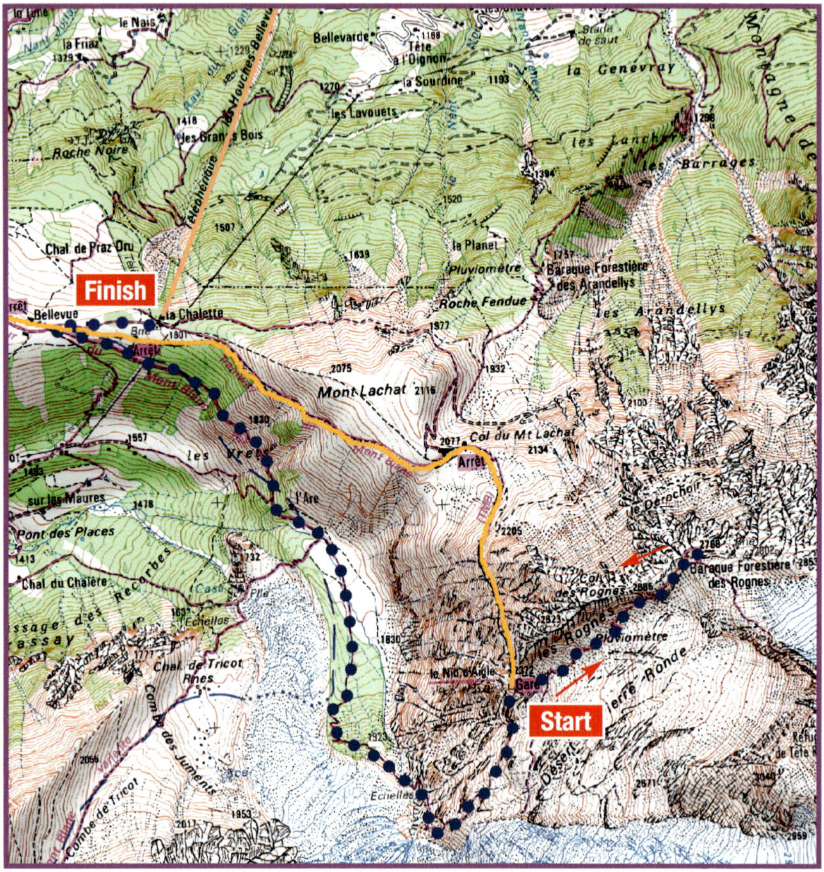

Altitude: 2,678 m
Level: Hiker
Schedule: Round trip Viewpoint of glacier 1 hour + Climb 1 hour 15 min to Baraque des Rognes + Descent 2 hours 15 min to Bellevue, allow 4 hours 30 min
Elevatio: Ascent 306 m + Descent 877 m
IGN 3531ET map or Pays du Mont-Blanc hiking map (A1 Rando Editions)
Access: top of the Bellevue-Les Houches gondola + Mont-Blanc Tramway station Nid d'Aigle.
Parking Les Houches-Bellevue cable car.

25 I Nid d'Aigle - Baraque des Rognes - Glacier de Bionnassay

High mountain environment for this hike that takes you to the Baraque des Rognes, a gateway for mountaineers seeking to conquer Mont-Blanc in the normal way. Unrestricted views of the Dôme du Goûter and its refuge, traces of mountaineers climbing to reach the top of Europe. The route back borders closely with the Bionnassay glacier at the foot of the magnificent peak named alike.

At the cable-car, head slightly downwards towards the Mont-Blanc de Bellevue Tramway station.
Take the Mont-Blanc Tramway to go towards Nid d'Aigle which is the terminus station.
Be careful to match the Bellevue cable schedules with the Mont-Blanc Tramway timetables.
Moreover, given the crowds at certain times, it is necessary to have a numbered card that indicates the train to catch.
Climb above the Nid d'Aigle station (2,372 m). You can start with a round trip to the glacier viewpoint by taking the path on the right.
Retrace your steps, then begin your climb on the steep and stony slopes leading to the Col des Rognes and its cabin. The trail winds its way up sharp bends in the arid desert valley of Pierre Ronde. After crossing the Col des Rognes, you reach the Baraque des Rognes ledge with many Ibex. Breathtaking views of the Aiguille du Goûter and its refuge.
Turn around and take the same route back to Nid d'Aigle.
Before getting to the Nid d'Aigle station, take the path that plunges to the left towards the right bank of the glacier and the valley of the Are.
The return begins with a sporty downhill trek on rocky slopes that run along the Bionnassay glacier and its moraine while dominating the impressive séracs and crevasses. The trail, which is sometimes overhead, is well equipped: two short passages on ladders, handrails and finally some metal steps allow to cross the rock face. Then the slope is gentler in the Are valley.
You cross a stream after the end of the glacier's tip. Leave the trail on the left going towards the Glacier's gateway and the Col du Tricot.
You get to the Are pastures and their cottages, at the entrance to the forest and the Bionnassay valley. Leave the trail on the left towards Bionnassay and continue through a wooded area, after crossing a small gate, to Bellevue station.

Vallée de Bionnassay

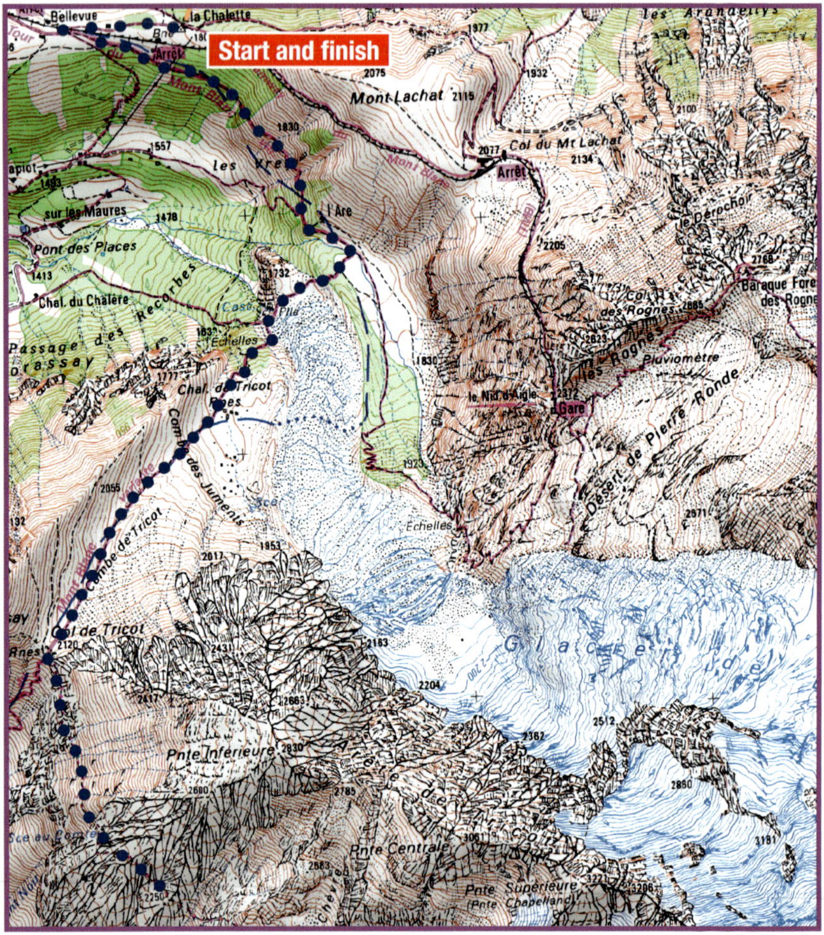

Altitude: 2,120 m
Level: Hiker
Schedule: Ascent 2 hours + Descent 2 hours
Elevation: 1,800 m to 2,120 m (ascent 430m + descent 430 m)
IGN 3531ET or Pays du Mont-Blanc hiking map (A1, Rando Editions)
Access: top of the Bellevue gondola at Les Houches
Parking Les Houches-Bellevue cable car.

26 I Col du Tricot from Bellevue (Les Houches)

A walk that takes you from valley to valley with views of: Chamonix, Bionnassay, Miage, Contamines-Montjoie and a breathtaking panorama of the Bionnassay glacier and the Miage domes.

At the cable car, head slightly downwards towards the Mont-Blanc Bellevue Tramway station and cross the tracks. The well sign posted trail leads into the forest to the pastures of the Are. At the first gate, continue straight through to a second gate. You get to a fork where you ignore on the left, a path that goes towards the Bionnassay glacier and the Mont-Blanc and Nid d'Aigle Tramway. By taking the winding trail to the right you reach a bridge suspended over the stream of the Bionnassay glacier (1,700 m). Breathtaking sight of the glacier, the Dôme du Goûter, the Aiguille de Bionnassay and the Mont-Blanc.

Cross the bridge, the trail first climbs through a forest and then quickly moves through a wide uncovered valley with a beautiful panorama. You can see the refuge of Tête Rousse and that of the Aiguille du Goûter which is the starting point to the classical way up the Mont-Blanc.

Once at the Col du Tricot, which is a focal point early in the climb, one dominates another valley with the Miage chalets below and on the same skyline just above, the Truc chalets. Panorama of 180° with the ski slopes of Contamines-Montjoie, the Montjoly, the Col du Bonhomme and on the left, the snow covered domes of Miage.

From the Col du Tricot, one can follow the trail on the left towards the Plan-Glacier refuge (which is not on the IGN map, but easy to follow), it is an overhanging trail on the Miage valley that allows different views of the Miage domes. One can stop along the way for a picnic, without trying to reach the refuge (2h30), because one must think of the way back, it is also much quieter here than at the Col du Tricot. Go back to the Col du Tricot, then take the route in reverse.

From the Col du Tricot:
Chalets de Miage (1,559 m): 1h20 (One way)
Truc Chalets (1,720 m): 1h55 (One way)
to Mont Vorassy: 0h30 (One way)
to Glacier Refuge (2,690 m): 2h30 (One way)

Valley of Bionnassay

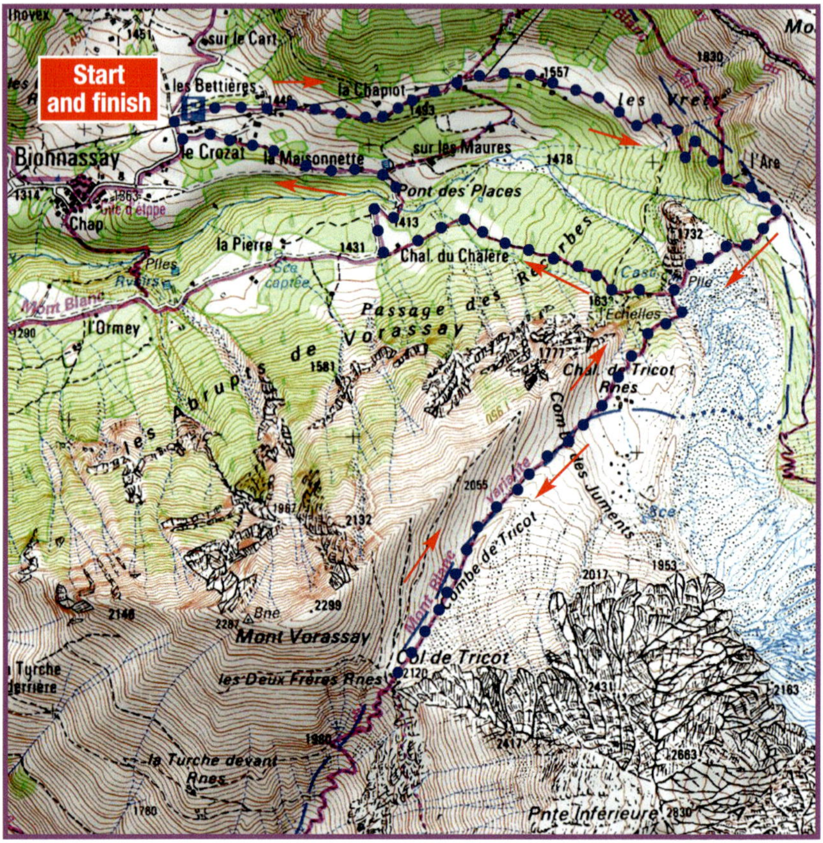

Altitude: 2,120 m
Level: Hiker
Time: 2 hours 45 min up + 1 hour 45 min down
Elevation: from 1,420 m to 2,120 m
Map: IGN 3531ET
Access: Le Crozat parking lot just above the village of Bionnassay. From Chamonix, take the N506 towards Saint-Gervais. Take exit 22 towards Saint-Gervais and then head to Les Contamines-Montjoie (D902). Near Bionnay, take the little street to the left that goes towards Bionnassay (it may be difficult to cross). Continue until you reach the parking lot at the end of the street. It should take about 1 hour.

27 I Col du Tricot from Bionnassay

A stroll that takes you from one valley to the next with various viewpoints along the way: Chamonix, Bionnassay, Miage, Contamines-Montjoie and an impressive view over the Bionnassay glacier and the Dômes de Miage peaks.

This hike allows you to reach Col du Tricot pass without taking the ski lifts at Bellevue (see Hike 26). Take the trail that starts to the right of the parking lot, headed towards Bellevue. The way is well marked and climbs up through the forest. You'll quickly reach (in 15 min) the Le Planet chalets (1,551m). In just under 1 hour, you'll reach the first fork at Are (1,760m). You'll pass a trail to your left that heads towards Col de Volza, Prarion, and Bellevue, and continue on towards Col du Tricot, Miage and Nid d'Aigle. Very quickly, you'll arrive in a valley where you'll already be able to see the Bionnassay glacier quite well as well as the sign for Are (1,760m) with a marked pathway to the left towards Nid d'Aigle, Bionnassay glacier. To the right you'll see our trail (marked "Col du Tricot, Chalets de Miage, Plan glacier") that descends in loops towards a suspension footbridge over the Bionnassay glacier stream (1,700 m). It's a breathtaking sight over the glacier, the Goûter peak, the Aiguille de Bionnassay and Mont Blanc.

Cross the footbridge. The trail will lead you up, first through forest and then fairly quickly into a valley with an incredible view.

You'll notice the Tête Rousse refuge and the Aiguille du Goûter refuge, the classic departure point for those heading up Mont Blanc.

Once at Col du Tricot pass, which you'll catch sight of quite early on in the hike, you'll overlook another valley: a valley with the Miage chalets below and, just above, the other Truc chalets. A 180° view of the ski tracks at Contamines-Montjoie, Mont Joly, Col du Bonhomme and, to the left, the snowy peaks of the Dômes de Miage.

After taking a moment to picnic, follow the itinerary back the way you came. In about 45 min you'll meet back up with the fork at "Glacier de Bionnassay" (1,760 m) before the footbridge. This time, head towards Bionnassay, Champet, Chalère to vary your trip on the way back.

The pathway descends into the forest (always follow the markings). You'll reach the Chalère chalets in about 1h15 min after Col du Tricot. At Chalère (1,431m), take the small road to the right towards Parking du Crozat, Bionnassay and cross the stream. Once you get to the fork at Le Pont des Places (1,413 m), head back up towards the parking lot at Crozat.

Valley of Bionnassay

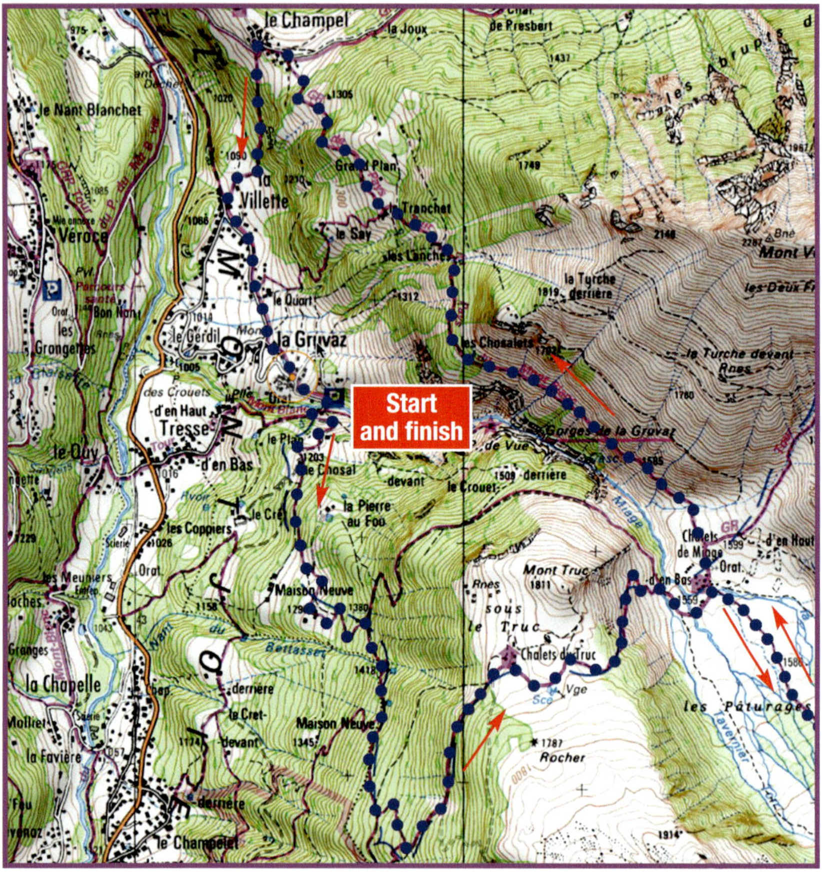

Altitude: 1,811 m
Level: Hiker
Time: 1 hour 30min up + 2 hours down (not including a side trip to the Plan glacier refuge)
Elevation: 1,090 m to 1,811 m (720 m up + 720 m down)
Map: IGN 3531ET
Access: From Chamonix, take the N 506 towards Saint-Gervais. Take exit 22 towards Saint-Gervais, then towards Contamines-Montjoie (D 902). After about 4 km, head left on the small road towards La Gruvaz (before the bridge crossing the stream). Continue along until you reach the parking lot at the end of the road. It should take about 45 min.

28 I Truc and Miage Chalets

A hike between forests, pastures, streams and glaciers, with chalets/ refuges easily accessible for a meal, a treat or a refreshment in front of the sumptuous decor of the northern glacier slopes of the Dômes de Miage.

This is a circular route. I suggest taking it in the following direction. From the Gruvaz parking lot (1,090 m), take the trail that heads up through the forest towards Chalets de Miage/ Le Truc (the time indicated is wrong). The trail climbs up to a first intersection at Le Chosal (1,203 m). Continue on towards Chalets de Miage / Chalets du Truc. At the Maison Neuve (1,380 m) crossing, head to the right towards the Truc chalets. At the Macherey intersection (1,585 m), you'll cross hikers coming from Contamines-Montjoie. Continue on towards the Truc chalets.

After 1h15 climbing through the forest, you'll leave the forest and start to see the Truc chalets in the middle of pastures. After the Truc refuge, there will be a viewpoint indicator to your right with a 180° view from Col du Tricot pass to the Aiguille de la Bérangère, passing by the Aiguille de Bionnassay and the Dômes de Miage.

Make a 20-min round-trip detour to the top of Mont Truc (1,811 m) on your left. You'll have a clear view over the Contamines-Montjoie Valley and you'll still be able to see the Miage glaciers. Go back down to the Miage chalets (1,555 m), which should take you about 30 min. You can picnic at the top of Mont Truc or in the pastures of Miage along the stream or even have lunch at the Miage refuge.

Coming from Miage, the Plan Glacier refuge (2,690 m) is about 3 hours away. You can take this itinerary for about 1 hr. After crossing the stream by a wooden footbridge, the trail leads gently up the Miage pastures over the right bank of the main stream, in front of the Dômes de Miage. It then heads up to a beautiful waterfall and then you'll find yourself on a passage with a handrail that leads you close to the stream. Magnificent view over the Miage valley and the Fiz mountain range.

Return via the same itinerary until you reach the Miage chalets. On your way back from Miage, you'll need 1h15 to get back down to the Gruvaz parking lot. Stay to the right of the stream on the Col de Tricot/Le Champel trail. You'll pass a trail on your right that goes towards Col de Tricot pass and continue on the mountainside trail that looks over the Gruvaz gorges. You'll also meet up with some forest and then the trail will slope steadily downwards through a forest of spruces. At the intersection of Le Cey (1,300 m), follow the signs for the Gruvaz parking lot (leave the trail, which continues on towards Le Champel).

Finally, you'll see the road to Gruvaz. Take the trail on your left just before you get to the road, that way you'll avoid having to head up the street to get to the parking lot.

Valley of Bionnassay

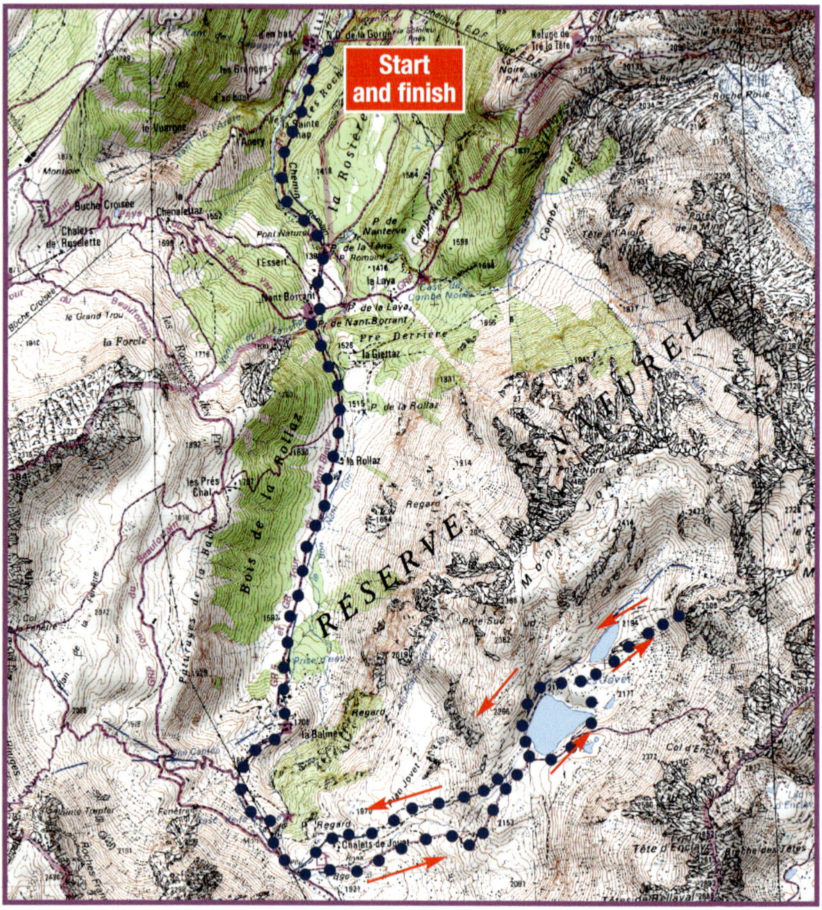

Altitude: 2,194 m
Level: Hiker
Time: 3 hours up + 2 hours 30 min down (not including a side trip to Mont Jovet)
Elevation: 1,210 m to 2,190 m (980 m)
Map: IGN 3531 ET
Access: From Chamonix, take the N 506 towards Saint-Gervais. Take exit 22 towards Saint-Gervais, then towards Contamines-Montjoie (D 902). Continue along the road until it ends at Notre-Dame-de-la-Gorge. It should take about 45 min.

29 I Jovet Lakes

A hike between forests, pastures, herds, streams, and lakes, with chalets/refuges easily accessible all along the way for a meal or refreshment. At the end, you'll reach the Jovet lakes at the heart of the Contamines-Montjoie nature reserve. A nature walk that goes beyond the TMB route, namely from the Jovet chalets to the Jovet lakes

From the parking lot, head towards the Notre Dame de la Gorge chapel. Go along the right bank of the stream, the ancient Roman road that heads up through the forest towards Col du Bonhomme pass (along the TMB). Follow the Tour du Mont Blanc (TMB) itinerary until you reach the Jovet chalets. After 30 min, while still in the forest, you'll reach a Roman bridge (1,425 m) with a beautiful waterfall. In the right season, the area is peppered with blueberries. When leaving the forest you'll see a wooden chalet, a relay-bar called "Le Sollié" and the Nant-Borrant refuge with its donkeys.

The wide path is uncovered and runs through the middle of pastures up until the Balme chalet/restaurant (1,706 m), which you'll reach in 1h30. You're halfway there.
Near the Jovet chalets, you'll leave the TMB and take a trail to the left towards the Jovet lakes. The landscape becomes wilder, with streams and waterfalls all along the way.
As you reach about 3 hours in, you'll see the first lake (2,174 m), which is also the largest, nestled at the bottom of an ancient glacial cirque and the foot of Mont Tondu. The second great lake (2,194 m) will reveal itself a bit beyond the end of the first lake. You can picnic on the edge of the lakes. After the second lake, I suggest you continue (turning around the lake to the right) following an unmarked dirt trail that climbs through a small, closed cirque by the Jovet Mountains. Continue on for about 30 min until you can see, when you turn around, the two lakes in their entirety. The view is truly worth it.
The brave of heart can continue along this grassy trail whose traces you can make out along the mountain flank to the left. Those who take this path will inevitably find a few groundhogs, whose shrieks you'll have been hearing now for some time. The trail ends on the crests of the Jovet mountains (2,428 m, plan for 1 hour to get there and 30 min on your way back from the lakes) with a beautiful view over the Montjoie Valley (if there's good visibility).
On the way back from the first lake, either take the same trail from the morning, along the left bank of the stream, or take the right bank trail, which is steeper and rockier and thus a bit less enjoyable on the way down. Both trails will take you to the Jovet chalets where you'll meet back up with the TMB. Plan for the descent to take 1 hour from the Jovet lakes until the Balme chalets. From the Balme chalets, you'll need another 30 min to reach the Nant-Borrant chalet/Le Sollié relay, and then another 30 min to arrive at the Notre-Dame-de-la-Gorge chapel.

Valley of Bionnassay

Altitude: 2,245 m (Col Fenêtre)
Level: Hiker
Time: 3 hours up + 2 hours down (loop)
Elevation: 450 m up
Map: IGN 3531 ET
Access: Gorge cable car parking lot, at the outskirts of the village of Contamines Montjoie. From Chamonix, take the N 506 towards Saint-Gervais. Take exit 22 towards Saint-Gervais, then towards Contamines Montjoie (D 902). The gorge cable car can be found on the right side after the Notre- Dame de la Gorge exit at Contamines. It should take about 40 min.

30 | The aiguille de Roselette - Col du Mont-Joly pass

This itinerary takes a loop around the Aiguille de Roselette, the GRP Tour of Beaufortin and its variant. There are two superb 360° views at the Col Fenêtre pass and the Col du Joly pass, with a viewpoint indicator that helps you find all the summits of the Mont Blanc mountain range.

Purchase a round-trip Gorge and Signal cable car ticket at the ski lift office. When you exit the station after arriving with the Signal cable car (1,850m), head to the left and take the trail towards "Les Prés" (it says it takes 1h20, but we'll get there in 1 hour).
The trail runs first through alpine pastures with a few low ups and downs. Beautiful view over the Contamines Montjoie Valley and the Dômes de Miage.
At the chalets (1,797 m), follow the sign for "Alpine pastures des Prés, Refuge de Balme, Col de la Fenêtre." A little further along, above the chalets, continue towards "Alpine pastures des Prés, Refuge de Balme" and then keep going towards "Plan Jovet, Refuge de Balme."

About 45 min after les Prés, leave the trail to take another trail on your right towards Col Joly, Col Fenêtre, Col de Gicle. The climb to Col Fenêtre pass starts out rather rustic. You'll meet up with it in about 1h15, taking a stone trail with fairly steep switchbacks at the end.
You can picnic at the pass where there is a superb, 360° view.
From here, switch to the other side of the trail for a descent overhanging Hauteluce valley where large herds of cattle, whose milk is used to make Beaufort cheese, frequent.
Just below the Col Fenêtre pass, head to your right following the signs for "Col du Joly." The trail overhangs alpine pastures all the way until "Sous l'Aiguille de Roselette," which you'll reach in 30 min. Very beautiful view over Mont Blanc.
Keep going towards "Tête du Lac de Roselette, Col du Joly."
At Col du Joly pass, which you'll reach in 35 min, there will be another extra large, 360° panorama with a viewpoint indicator. On one side you'll see Beaufortin and, on the other, Mont Blanc and all its summits.
You'll then need 20 min to join back up with the Signal cable car below the Col du Joly, with Lake Roselette on your right.

Valley of Bionnassay

Altitude: 3,167 m
Level: Hiker
Time: 2 hours 15 min up + 1 hour 45 min down
Elevation: Nid d'Aigle (2,372 m) to Tête Rousse (3,167 m), a 795 m climb
Map: IGN 3531ET or Pays du Mont Blanc hiking map (A1, Rando edition)
Access: top of the Bellevue cable car at Les Houches + Mont Blanc Tramway (TMB), Bellevue to Nid d'Aigle station
Les Houches-Bellevue ski-lift parking lot (few spaces) or at Le Prarion

31 I Nid d'Aigle - Tête Rousse Refuge

High mountain ambiance during this hike that passes by the shelter at Rognes and leads you to the Tête Rousse refuge, a point of passage for mountain climbers on a quest to reach Mont Blanc by the normal route. Breathtaking views of the Goûter peak and its refuge. It's the climber's trail in pursuit of Europe's rooftop. Many ibex along the way.

When you reach the cable car, head slightly downwards to the TMB station at Bellevue. Take the TMB to get to Nid d'Aigle, the final station.

Be sure to check that the Bellevue cable car hours and the TMB hours match up (www.compagniedumontblanc.fr). Free spaces for the Bellevue stop are provided on the first two trains of the day. As soon as you get to Nid d'Aigle, ask for a card with your preferred return time.

Start your climb on the steep and rocky slopes that lead to the Col des Rognes and a forest cabin (2,768 m). The trail climbs in tight switchbacks up the arid valley of the Pierre Ronde desert. After passing the Col des Rognes, you'll meet back up with (1 hour after Nid d'Aigle) the shelter at Rognes and numerous ibex. You'll need about another 1h15 to reach the Tête Rousse refuge. You'll first cross Plat des Rognes and then head up in loops to the Payot arête– there are several areas with handrails along the way. This climb is not recommended for people with vertigo.

All along the climb you'll have a breathtaking view of the north face of the Aiguille de Bionnassay and the Aiguille du Goûter with its new refuge on the edge of a huge drop-off. There are also a few nice views over the Aiguille du Midi on the left.

Finally, you'll reach a crossing: the last cliff before a small glacier. Depending on the weather, you may decide to use equipment to cross over to the glacier and meet back up with the Tête Rousse refuge.

Picnic at the refuge while watching the ropes heading towards the Goûter refuge (3863m). The way to Mont Blanc's summit (4,810m) is still quite far, and it starts with the dangerous passageway at the Aiguille du Goûter.

The way back takes you along the same itinerary. Plan for 1 hour from the shelter at Rognes + 40 min for the Nid d'Aigle.

Valley of Bionnassay

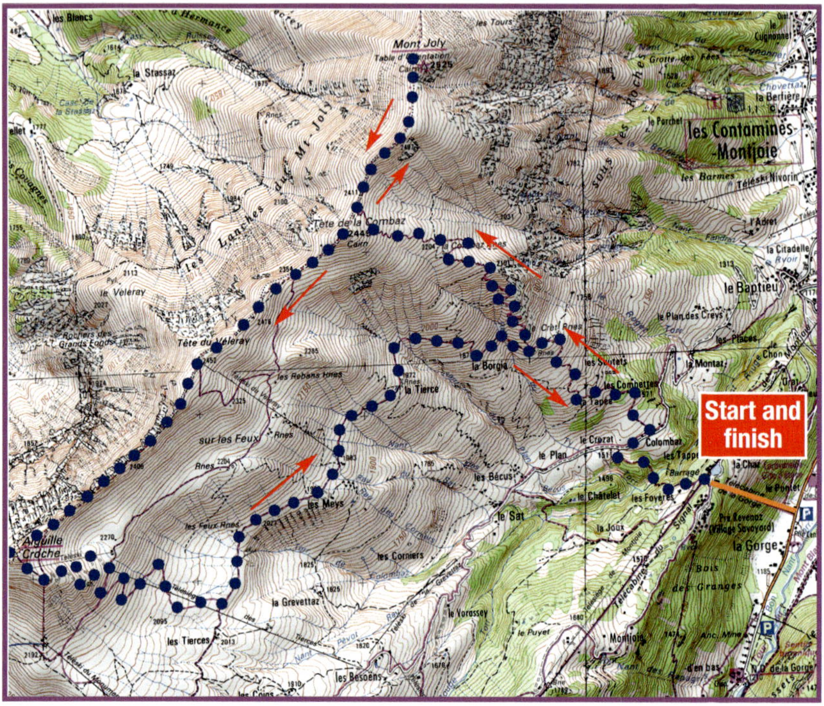

Altitude: 2,525 m (Mont-Joly)
Level: Experienced Hiker
Time: 3 hours up + 3 hours 30 min back, in a loop
Elevation: 1,045 m up to Mont-Joly
Map: IGN 3531 OT or Pays du Mont Blanc hiking map (A1, Rando edition)
Access: Gorge cable cars parking lot at the outskirts of the village of Contamines-Montjoie. From Chamonix, take the N 506 towards Saint-Gervais. Take exit 22 towards Saint-Gervais, then towards Contamines Montjoie (D902). The Gorge cable cars will be on your right after the Notre-Dame de la Gorge exit for Contamines. It should take about 40 min.
The Gorge cable cars run in July/August from 8:45am to 5:30pm (double check the times). Note: for those who don't wish to be tied down by the cable car hours or who plan to go outside of the opening times, you can do this hike from the hamlet of Baptieu (1,179 m) but it will take a bit longer and the difference in elevation will be somewhat more significant.

32 I Mont Joly mountain range

A challenging, circular route with an aerial part (not recommended for people with vertigo– this hike is only for good weather days) over the ridge of Mont Joly at the Aiguille Croche. There's an exceptional 360° panoramic view at Mont-Joly with a viewpoint indicator that helps you to identify all the summits of the Mont Blanc mountain range.

Purchase a round-trip ticket at the ski lift office to take the Gorges cable car for the first section, up to Étape (1,480 m).
When you exit the cable car at Signal (1,850 m), take the trail marked "Colombaz." It's best not to arrive at Signal later than 9:30am if you plan to do the whole loop. The trail heads down through the forest, then crosses a stream before heading back up via a forest road all the way to Colombaz (1,500 m), which you'll reach in about 15 min.
The trail then climbs up a steep, uncovered slope through the pastures and crosses over an area with a watering hole, called "La Tappée" (1,630 m), and a place called "Pré Conduit" (1,830 m), which you'll reach about 1 hour after the initial departure. At the intersection, take the trail to the right marked "Tête de la Combaz / Mont-Joly." The climb continues unabated towards the Tête de la Combaz (2,445 m), situated above the ridge, which you'll reach in about 2h30 after the initial departure. The fruits of your labor: a magnificent view.

It won't take more than 30 min of walking along the ridge trail to the right (a rather wide trail) to reach Mont Joly (2,525 m) and an extra large 360° panoramic view and viewpoint indicator. You can picnic here.
For the way back, take the ridge trail backwards until you get to La Combaz. Follow the ridge until you get to Tête du Veleray (2,452 m) and, finally, until the foot of the Aiguille Croche, where you'll arrive in less than 1h30. Consider stopping to admire the splendid landscape and don't forget that you're walking along a mountain ridge. Bird's eye view over the Megève airfield on one side, and, of course, the Mont Blanc mountain range on the other.
Leave from the bottom of the Aiguille Croche around 3pm at the latest so you don't miss the last cable car. Head towards the plateau below you via the path to your left (do not go towards Col du Joly). If you head down quickly, it should take about 1h30 to reach Colombaz. In 45 min you'll be at Meys (1,970 m) and in 1h15 you'll be at Pré Conduit (1,830 m) where you can meet back up with the trail you took in the morning. You'll need just 30 min to get back to the cable car at Étape, taking the same path from the morning (marked "Les Tappes").

Sector of Anterne

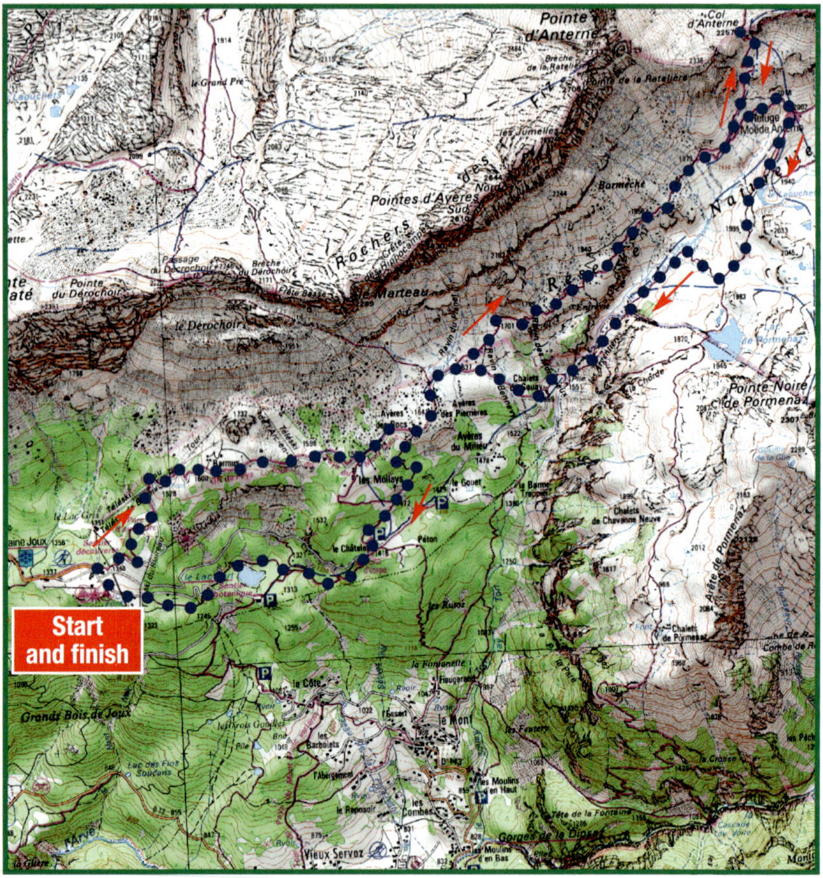

Altitude: 2,257 m
Level: Hiker
Schedule: Ascent 2 hours 30 min - Descent 2 hours 30 min
Elevation: Ascent 839 m + Descent 839 m
Map: Pays du Mont-Blanc hiking map (A1, Rando Editions)
Access: Plaine-Joux Parking (1st parking, departure area for para gliders)
From Chamonix, take the N 506 towards Saint-Gervais, exit n° 22, direction Passy then Plateau d'Assy then Plaine Joux, allow 45 minutes.
Moëde-Anterne Refuge.

33 I Col d'Anterne, Lac de Pormenaz

This hike is done in the heart of the Passy Nature Reserve with the Mont-Blanc, the Aravis and the Fiz Rocks in the background. A day of tranquility that will appeal to lovers of wide panoramas.

Park your car at the 1st parking of Plaine-Joux at the tee of para gliders (the road continues to the 2nd parking lot of Lac Vert).
From the car park, head to the ski lift (on the left when you arrive from Plateau d'Assy) then take the gravel path of the Tour du Pays du Mont-Blanc (TPMB) towards "Les Mollays". The path runs along the edge of the forest and you quickly reach the clear, flowery mountain pasture of the Mollays (1,580 m) with its pastoral views of the Mont-Blanc. Continue the TPMB towards the Chalets des Ayères (1,641 m) which is reached in 30 minutes. You join a track which passes over the chalets towards the Col d'Anterne Refuge. The climb on this track (still TPMB) that winds under the Fiz Rocks and leads to the Col d'Anterne refuge is a little tedious. Within 2 hours, one reaches a junction just before the Col d'Anterne Refuge that can be seen on the right. Take the path on the left towards the Col d'Anterne. After a very steep climb of about 30 minutes, you arrive at the pass (2,257 m). From the pass, the view is 360°, on one side the Mont-Blanc, on the other you can see the emerald green Anterne Lake below, largest lake in Savoie, and the Anterne pastures with their sheep. The Anterne pass is a beautiful gazebo with unobstructed views, suitable for a picnic. From the Col d'Anterne, you can make a round trip to Lake Anterne (2,063 m) by adding 1 hour). Turn around and go back down to the Col d'Anterne refuge (2,002 m).
From the refuge, the Fiz massif fortress with its multilayers of limestone is remarkable. Continue towards Lac de Pormenaz (1,945 m), reached in 30 minutes. The lake is surrounded by diverse flora and it is not uncommon for people to swim. From there, to go down to Plaine-Joux, retrace your steps towards the Anterne pass refuge then take the first path on your left towards the Chalets du Souay (arrows "Les Argentières"). The steep path declines rapidly down to the stream of Souay which is crossed by a footbridge before joining the chalets (1,569 m). At the Ayères chalets you can join the path taken in the morning that leads back to Plaine-Joux by Mollays or continue the descent to the Middle Ayères, the Chatelet and join the emerald and transparent waters of the Lac Vert. From Lac Vert, go back to the panoramic parking of Plaine-Joux.

Sector of Anterne

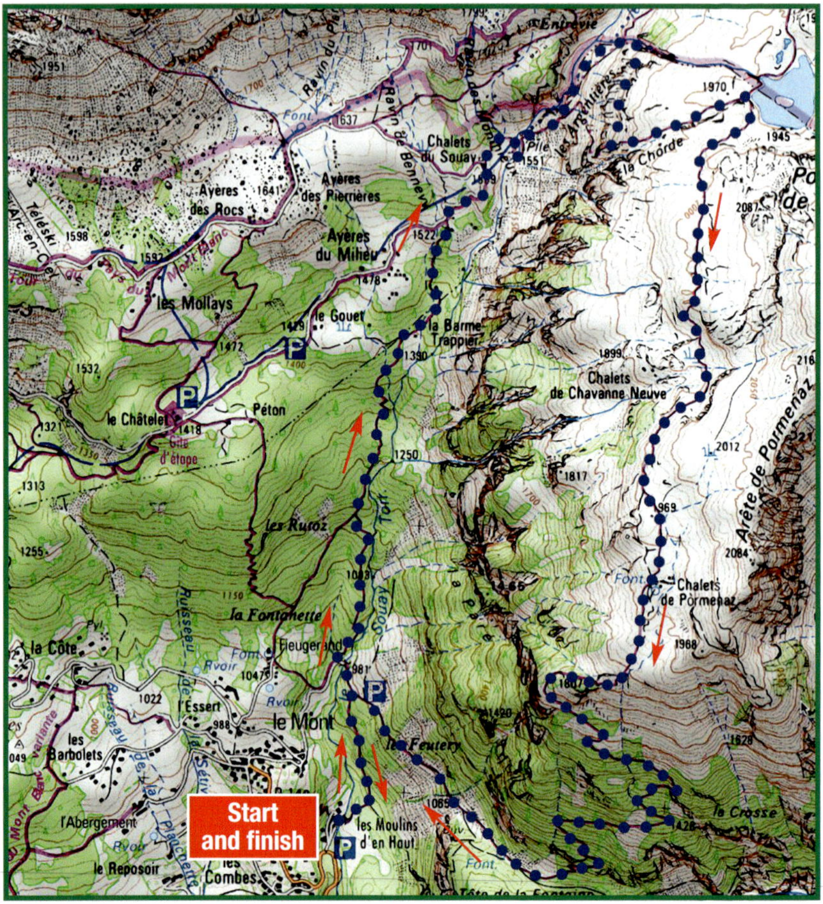

Altitude: 1,945 m Lac de Pormenaz
Level: Hiker
Time: 3 hours up - 3 hours 15 min down
Elevation: 1,080 m (from 865 m at the parking lot to 1,945 m at Lac de Pormenaz)
Map: IGN 3530 ET or Pays du Mont Blanc hiking map at 1/50 000, A1 edition
Access: Les Moulins d'en Haut parking lot above Servoz.
From Chamonix, take the N 506 towards Saint-Gervais. Exit at Servoz. It should take about 20 minutes.

34 I Le lac de Pormenaz from Servoz

**At the heart of the Passy nature reserve you'll find Lake Pormenaz. Overhung by the imposing Pointe Noire of Pormenaz and the Rochers des Fiz, for nature lovers this is an essential, must-see nature walk.
You'll also discover the old Pormenaz Alpine chalets, which are still inhabited by shepherds and their herds of sheep.**

The trail starts at the parking lot and climbs along the Souay river. You'll quickly reach the Chouay bridge (981m).
Follow the path that heads through the forest full of mushrooms and it will lead you in just 1h45 to the chalets of Souay (1,569 m).
Cross the river at the footbridge below the chalets and head towards Lake Pormenaz via the La Chorde pass. The very steep trail climbs at an intense incline and some areas are equipped with cables and ladders. It leads you in 1h15 directly to the lake where you can picnic.

The lake is surrounded by diverse flora and it's not uncommon for some visitors to take a quick dip in the water. From the lake, you can't help but notice the fortress of the Fiz mountain chain and its stacks of limestone. Return by the Chavanne Neuve chalets and then the Pormenaz chalets.
From the lake, be sure to follow the unmarked dirt path that leads between damp ledges and puddles. You'll quickly see a path to your left leading to Pointe Noire de Pormenaz (1h15 from the lake, marked in yellow).
After 45 min, you'll see the Mont Blanc mountain range and, below you, the Pormenaz chalets and Alpine pasture with numerous sheep.
In 2h15(after the lake), you'll reach an area called "La Fontaine" (1,135 m). Take a 15 min detour to the view of Tête de la Fontaine's chalet refreshment area (1,206 m) where you can have a drink on the terrace overlooking Servoz. There's a panoramic view over the Fiz and Aravis mountains, the villages of Cordon and Combloux, and the Domancy plains.
There's just 45 min left to head back down to the parking lot, passing by le Mont.
If you're not too tired, take the opportunity to discover the old village of Servoz, an authentic and traditional mountain village with old chalets and farms. Or, why not visit Gorges de la Diosaz? (http://www.gorgesdeladiosaz.com/)

Sector of Anterne

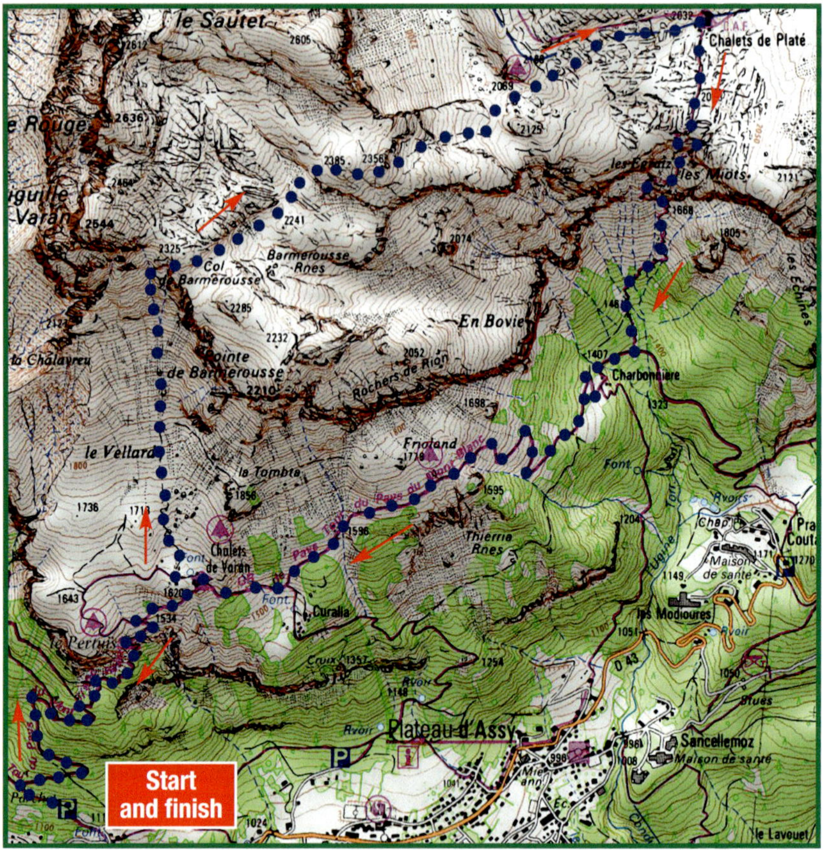

Altitude: 2,325 m at Col de Barmerousse
Level: Experienced Hiker
Time: around 7 hours for the loop
Elevation: from 1,200 m (parking lot) to 2,325 m (Col de Barberousse)
Map: IGN 3530 ET or Pays du Mont Blanc hiking map at 1/50 000, A1 edition
Access: Coudray parking lot at Bay.
From Chamonix, take the N 506 towards Saint-Gervais. Take exit 21 towards Passy, then Plateau d'Assy, then Bay. It should take about 40 minutes.
Chalet de Varan (1,620 m) - Refuge de Platé (2,032 m)

35 | From Varan to Platé via the Col de Barmerousse pass

An athletic hike through the Platé Desert, the largest mineral desert in Europe. The two refuges, Varan and Platé, are old Alpine pasture chalets located along the Tour des Fiz.
A day in nature with large, contrasting views of the Fiz mineral chain and the Mont Blanc mountains and glaciers.

From the parking lot, the hike starts with a forest trail that you'll leave behind to take a shortcut to the right just 10 min before the Varan chalets. In 1 hour, you'll reach a refuge situated to the far west on the south side of the Fiz chain, leaning against the flank of the Aiguille de Varan. This refuge overlooks the Arve valley and the plains of Sallanches, facing the Mont Blanc mountain range.

Take a break at the refuge before attacking the steep climb up Vellard, directly above the chalets and headed in the direction of the Aiguilles de Varan and the Col de Barmerousse pass. The steady, uphill climb takes you on a rocky, winding trail that allows you to reach the pass in about 1h30 after leaving the refuge. Views over the Aiguille de Varan (2,544 m) and the Aiguille Rouge (2,637 m). Ibex along the way. From the pass, start crossing the Platé Desert by taking an off-trail route marked by red points on rock slabs, laid down and covered in holes (limestone). Give yourself about 2 hours from the pass to the Platé refuge. Choose one of the upcoming valleys to picnic at. Then, continue along the itinerary towards the Platé refuge. Soon you'll see the arrival of a chairlift from Flaine and, below, the refuge with its blue shutters and sheep.

Take a break at the refuge before starting the descending "Egratz," which will take you along a steep trail surrounded by shale where you'll have to watch your step. After 1h15 downhill, you'll reach a fork at the Ugine River (1,389 m). Do not go towards Plaine Joux/ Praz-Coutant. Rather, head to your right towards the Chalets de Curalla / Chalets de Varan. The climb up at the end of the day towards the Varan refuge is a bit challenging. You'll need about 45 minutes. Drink a refreshing and well-deserved beverage at the Varan refuge before heading back to the trail you took in the morning for the last 45 minutes descent.

It's also possible to hike this loop from the Praz-Coutant parking lot (1,171 m), located halfway between Plateau d'Assy and Plaine Joux. The benefit would be to take on all the uphill stretches in the morning.

Swiss mountainside

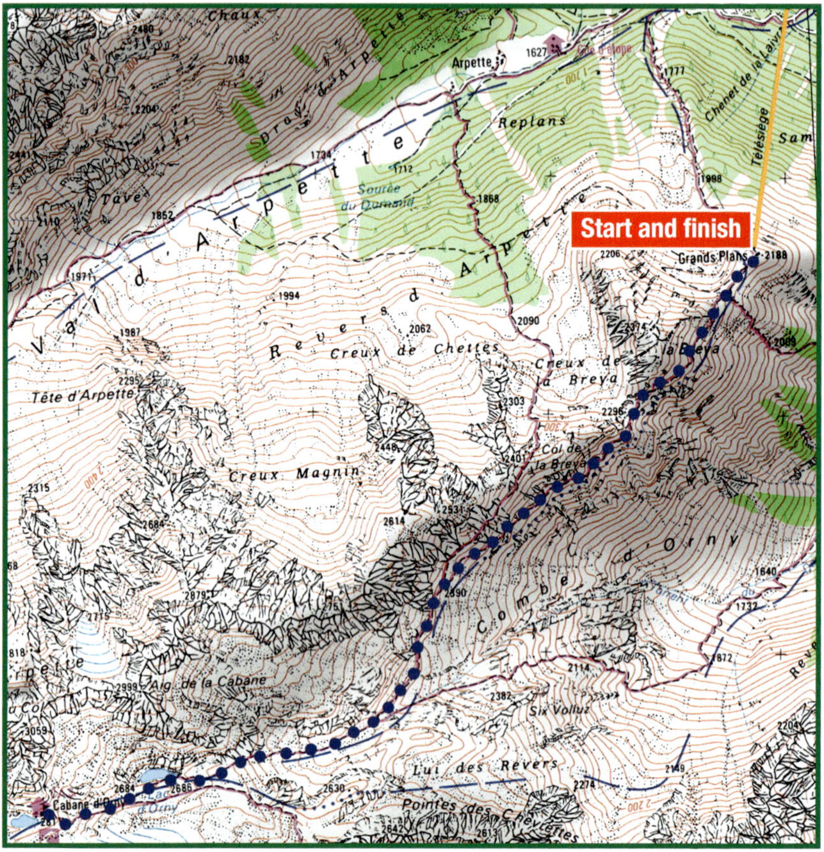

Altitude: 2,811 m
Level: Hiker
Schedule: Ascent 2 hours 15 min + Descent 1 hour 30 min
Elevation: 2,188 m to 2,811 m
IGN map 3630 OT or Pays du Mont-Blanc hiking map (A1, Rando Editions)
Access: car park Breya chairlift at Champex-le-Lac in Switzerland
From Chamonix, N506 towards Argentière. Cross the Swiss border, direction Col de Forclaz; go to Martigny then right on the road the Grand-Saint-Bernard, right again to Champex-le-Lac; allow about one hour to Cabane d'Orny, guarded refuge from mid-June to mid-September.

36 I Cabane d'Orny

A long and pleasant upward journey that leads to the Orny glacier and its refuge just before reaching the high mountains. A trail seldom used with distant views to the highest peaks in Switzerland visible beyond the valley.

Take the Breya chairlift that takes you 700 meters further up.
At the chairlift, go left, then take the path toward the Orny cabin. At the end of this pleasant but slightly steep trail, you reach a junction. Continue on your way, ignoring the path on the right which comes from Champex by the Breya pass.
Within an hour, you reach a second junction. Continue straight on ignoring the path on the left which comes from the Combe d'Orny. You cross a plateau and the path winds through large fallen rocks. In 1h45 minutes you reach Orny lake
on the right then the left bank of the moraine of Orny glacier, while on the left is the path leading to the Arpette Saleina Vallon.

Follow the moraine to the superior lake of Orny situated below the Cabane d'Orny.
The Cabane d'Orny is a refuge, the beginning of the high mountain and glacier hikes leading to the Trient cabin and the tip of Orny, a hike reserved for experienced hikers and equipped with the proper equipment for walking on a glacier.
You can picnic at the Cabane d'Orny.
The way down is via the same route as the one taken in the morning but staying to the left of the two successive junctions. At the 3rd junction, two options are available to you; either take the path on the right taken in the morning which joins the Breya chairlift (check the return schedules) ; or take a left towards the Breya pass and the Val d'Arpette. If you choose the latter route, add one hour for the way down to Champex.
On the return, take the opportunity to visit Champex-Lac, which is a quiet resort in the enchanting site of the alpine lake of Champex and a major stage of the Tour du Mont-Blanc.

Swiss mountainside

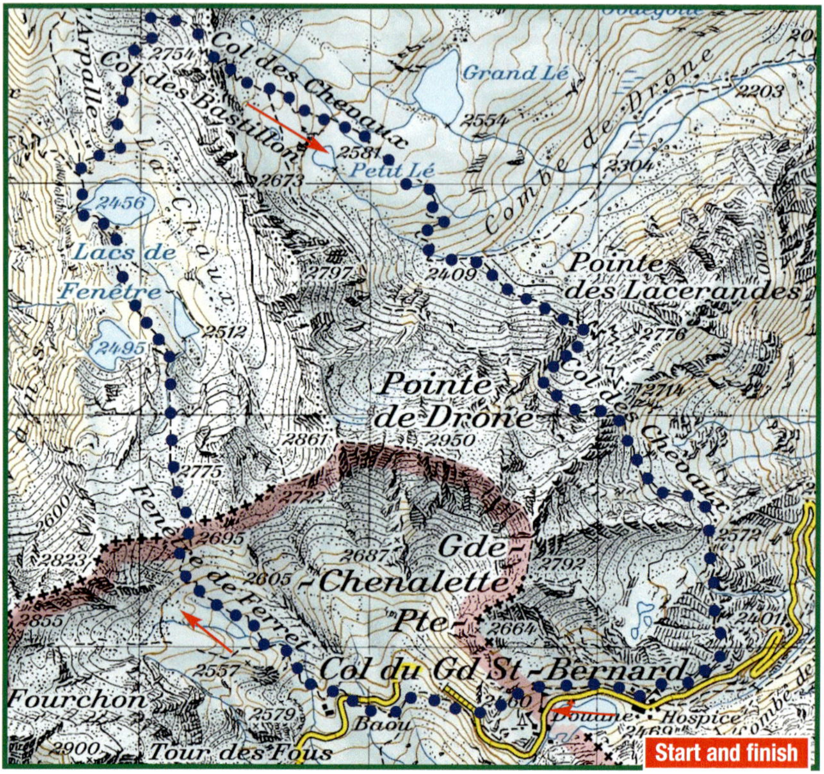

Altitude: 2,194 m
Level: Hiker
Time: 2 hours from Hospice (2,468 m) to Lacs de Fenêtre (2,456 m) passing by the Fenêtre de Ferret (2,698 m)
2 hours 30 min from Lacs de Fenêtre (2,456 m) to Hospice (2,468 m), passing by Col de Bastillon (2,761 m) and Col des Chevaux (2,700 m)
Map: (Note that on the Swiss map the "Col de Bastillon" is called "Col des Chevaux" and the "Col des Chevaux" is called "Pas des Chevaux")
Access: Grand-Saint-Bernard hospice at the Switzerland-Italy border.From Chamonix, head towards Argentière (N506). Cross the Swiss border while heading towards Col de la Forclaz.Go all the way to Martigny, and then take the Grand-Saint-Bernard road to the right. After Bourg-Saint-Pierre, just before the Grand-Saint-Bernard tunnel, turn right towards Col du Grand-Saint-Bernard. Follow the road until you get to the Grand-Saint-Bernard hospice and park there. It should take about 1h20.

37 I Fenêtre Lakes

A circular hike leaving from the Grand-Saint-Bernard hospice and passing by the Fenêtre de Ferret (a pass), the three Fenêtre lakes, the Col du Bastillon pass and, last but not least, the Col des Chevaux pass. The Fenêtre lakes are three magnificent expanses of water that culminate at a height of 2,456 m, situated in a world full of minerals. This hike also offers views over the most beautiful Swiss and Italian Alp summits.

This is a circular route. Along the way, there are a succession of ups and downs as you cross three passes: Fenêtre, Bastillon and Chevaux. The length of the hike is about the same on the way there as on the way back. However, the direction proposed here allows for an easier time climbing up and, above all, it will take you downhill towards the hospice at the end, thus keeping you from having to go uphill at the end of the hike.

Park your car at the hospice parking lot. Head towards the Plan de Jupiter (the giant statue) then take the ancient Roman road in order to reach the start of the Fenêtre lakes hike below, via Fenêtre de Ferret.

Although the start of the hike is fairly difficult to find (Baus' hospice-farm path below the route, on the Italian side, which you'll reach in about 20 min), the rest of the route is well marked. Start your hike up to the Col Fenêtre de Ferret pass (it's marked "13A), which you'll reach in 1 hr and which marks the border between Italy and Switzerland. From Fenêtre de Ferret, you'll head quickly down to the lakes in just 30 min. The second lake on the left is splendid with its blue color and, in the background, the Italian side of Mont Blanc. You can picnic at the lakes, but don't stay too long– there's a long trip ahead! After passing the third lake, take a path to the right to start tackling the very steep climb to the Col du Bastillon, which you'll reach in 45 min. All along the climb, the view of the three lakes and the Italian side of the Mont Blanc mountain chain is superb. There's a somewhat aerial passage as you arrive at the pass.

From the Col du Bastillon, there's a huge descent through a large, grassy hollow. Once in the valley, take the pathway to the right that goes up towards the Col des Chevaux. You'll need 1h15 to go from the Col de Bastillon to the Col des Chevaux. At the Col des Chevaux, there will be another magnificent view. Finally, take 30 min to head down towards the hospice.

For those who want to take a round-trip to the lake via Fenêtre de Ferret in around 2h45, park your car past the hospice on the route below the Switzerland/Italy border and close to the Baus Alpine pastures farm.

Swiss mountainside

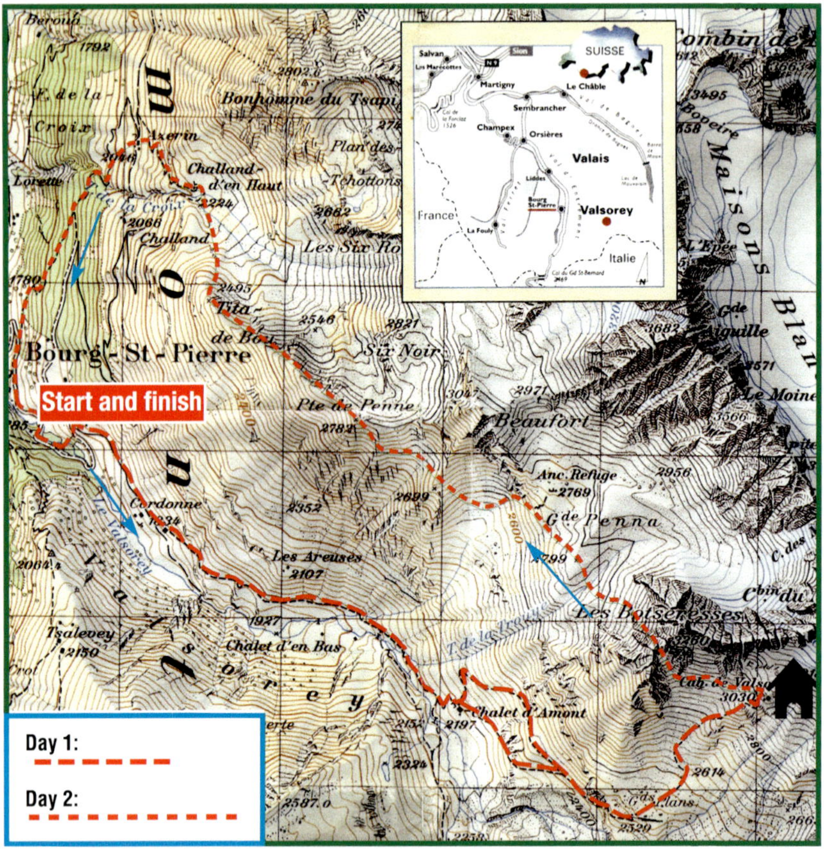

Altitude: 3,030 m (Cabane Valorsey)
Level: Experienced Hiker
Time: 3 hours 30 min (Day 1) + 5 hours 30 min (Day 2)
Circular route. Map above.
Access: Bourg Saint Pierre along the Grand-Saint-Bernard road in Switzerland. From Chamonix, head towards Argentière (N 506) and cross the Swiss border in the direction of Col de Forclaz. Go until Martigny and then take a right on to Grand-Saint-Bernard road. Park at the entrance to Bourg-Saint-Pierre near the Charmettes hostel. It should take around 1 hour 10 min.
Reserve room + half board (breakfast + dinner) before starting your hike: http://www.valsorey.ch

38 | Cabane Valsorey

Cabane Valsorey (the Valsorey Cabin) is situated along the southwest flank of the Grand Combin in the Swiss Valais, on a rocky outcrop facing Mont Velan.
A new trail allows you to climb down from the cabin along a beautiful, panoramic route with the Mont Blanc mountain chain in view.

This circular itinerary takes 2 days. It's a well-marked router that should only be undertaken during good weather. The hike to the cabin can also be done in one day by taking the Day 1 itinerary both there and back, but that means missing the scenic trails of Day 2.

Day1

The trail begins in the Bourg-Saint-Pierre village, in front and to the left of the church. Follow the yellow / black markings for around 15 min until you get to a crossing with an asphalt road near Plan du Pey (1,827 m) where you'll see red / white markings begin. The trail climbs sideways up part of the Entremont Valley, gaining more than 800 m in height between the village (1,689 m) and Grands Plans (2,529 m).

You'll first head towards the Cordonna Alpine pastures (1,934 m) on a trail that snakes through the middle of Alpine flora along the border of the Valsorey River's right bank.
At 45 min, after passing Chalets d'en Bas, you'll cross a branch of the river and then continue on the trail without crossing the main river (itinerary for heavy rains).
At 1h15, you'll pass a path on your right that leads to Cabane Velan (the Velan cabin) on the left side of the river.
Above the Chalets d'Amont (2,197 m), the trail begins to climb rapidly up.
At 1h45, you'll reach the shoulder and shift to the other side from where you can see the glacier. The trail continues along until you reach a fork– always stay to the left on your way to Cabane Valsorey (on the right there's yet another route heading to Cabane Velan).
At 2h15, you'll reach a large flat area (Grands Plans 2,529 m) from where you can see the cabin perched on its rock, with a view over the southern face of the Grand Combin.
You'll still need more than 1 hour to reach the cabin after a difficult climb up a steep slope (500 m up). From the cabin, there's a magnificent view over the Valsorey glacier, Mont Velan and the Alps. Enjoy the sunset over the Alps and at the horizon over Mont Blanc, if it's not in the clouds.
Note that the cabin is the departure point of those climbing up Combin de Valsorey (4,184 m) and then Grand Combin (4,314 m) via the Meitin arête.
Also note: the cabin is situated along the most demanding leg, a variant of the Haute Route, which connects Chamonix to Zermatt.

Day 2

The panoramic trail begins a bit below the cabin. Head towards Challand d'en Haut. Be careful to follow the markings (on the rocks) for this first part, as the trail travels along a sheer edge through scree for about 1 hr in order to avoid the rocky bar at Botderesses.
Next, you'll find a more clearly marked trail that descends close to the ancient Penna refuge (2,769 m), climbs up a peak of the same name (2,782 m) and runs along a ridge towards Tita de Bou (2,495 m), which you'll reach in about 4 hours.
You can picnic here since afterwards you'll change sides and will no longer have the exceptional 180° view of the glaciers and Alps that you've been seeing since you left in the morning.
An impressive descent takes you, in less than 1 hour, to the Challand d'en Haut (2,224 m) where you will find Alpine pastures and cows. Continue along, without crossing the river, in the direction of Azerin (it says 25 min).
After 15 min, don't be like me and follow the rather tempting signs for Bourg-Saint-Pierre, Plan du Pey, which will take you in 1 hour to Bourg-Saint-Pierre via a road followed by another road that descends through an airy forest. Rather, continue following the signs for Azerin (2,046 m), as indicated on the map, where you should find a trail to the left to complete the loop and take you back to Bourg-Saint-Pierre.

Swiss mountainside

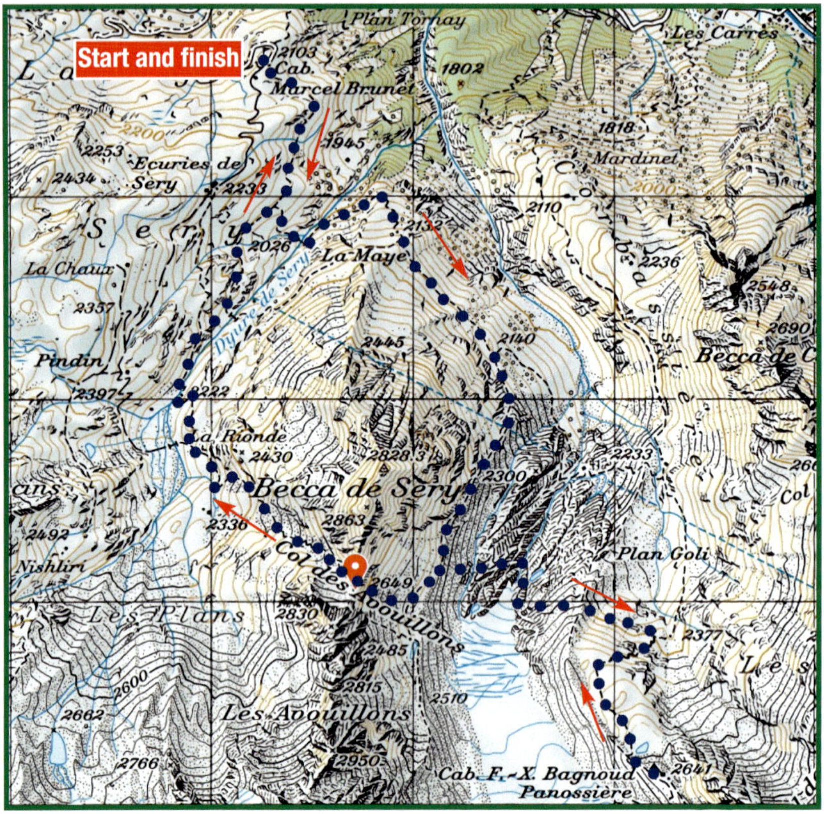

Altitude: 2,641 m
Level: Hiker
Time: 2 hours 30 min there + 3 hours back
Elevation: 2,103 m to 2,641 m
Map above.
Access: It should take about 1h30 from Chamonix. Head towards Argentière (N 506) and cross the Swiss border in the direction of Col de Forclaz. Keep going until Martigny and then take a right on Grand-Saint-Bernard road, then a left towards Verbier. At Verbier, take a right on the Mauvoisin dam road.
After Lourtier and before you get to Fionnay, take a small, narrow road to the right marked "Cabane Brunet" which will lead you in 15 min to a parking lot. (Warning: there are limited parking spaces.)

39 I Cabane Panossière

A circular route from the Cabane Brunet (Brunet cabin) to the Cabane Panossière (Panossière cabin), at the foot of the Corbassière glacier in the wonderful area of Combins. This hike presents a rural setting surrounded by flowers all the way until the Corbassière bridge, where you'll start to see high mountains and glaciers. The Djure de Corbassière crossing, via a 70 m high and 200 m long suspended bridge, can be somewhat overwhelming for people with vertigo.

On the way, the well marked (red and white) trail runs by a leg of the Tour des Combins. The trail starts to the left of Cabane Brunet. After 35 min, you'll pass another trail on your right that leads to the Col des Avouillons pass. Go to the left towards a small footbridge that crosses the Dyure de Sery. A bit more than 1 hour later keep going straight on the path (towards the Col des Avouillons via the Corbassière footbridge). After a steep climb, you'll catch a glimpse of the Corbassière glacier and the footbridge at its base below.

Take a pause before crossing the footbridge that passes over tumultuous waters escaping the glacier. You've still got a good climb up to the cabin (35-45 min depending on what shape you're in). To the right of the footbridge there's a little blue lake where some people like to take a dip. To your right you'll see the petit Combin and, behind the glacier, the grand Combin (4,314 m). Picnic (or have lunch) at the cabin, by the impressive view of the glacier and the Combins cirque. On the way back, take the same itinerary as you did on your way there up until the suspended footbridge (30 min), which you'll need to cross back over. Take on the climb towards the Col des Avouillons: a first, steep 20 min will take you to a small flat area and a second steep part will take you to the pass, which you'll reach in about 1 hour in total from the footbridge. Take a break at the pass and enjoy the view of the Combins glacier and mountains one last time.

Now you'll start your descent and return through fields, accompanied by the cries of marmots.

You'll see black cows below you and a sheepfold that you'll reach in 30 min. You'll see all kinds of flowers whose names I do not know: white ones, yellow ones, pink ones, purple ones... 45 min after leaving the pass, you'll cross back over the Dyure river. A bit further along (15 min), you'll reach the footbridge you crossed that morning. You may be feeling tired, but there are still another 30 min left to reach Cabane Brunet via a slightly uphill trail. Before you arrive at the cabin, be sure to catch the view over Lake Fionnay below you.

Swiss mountainside

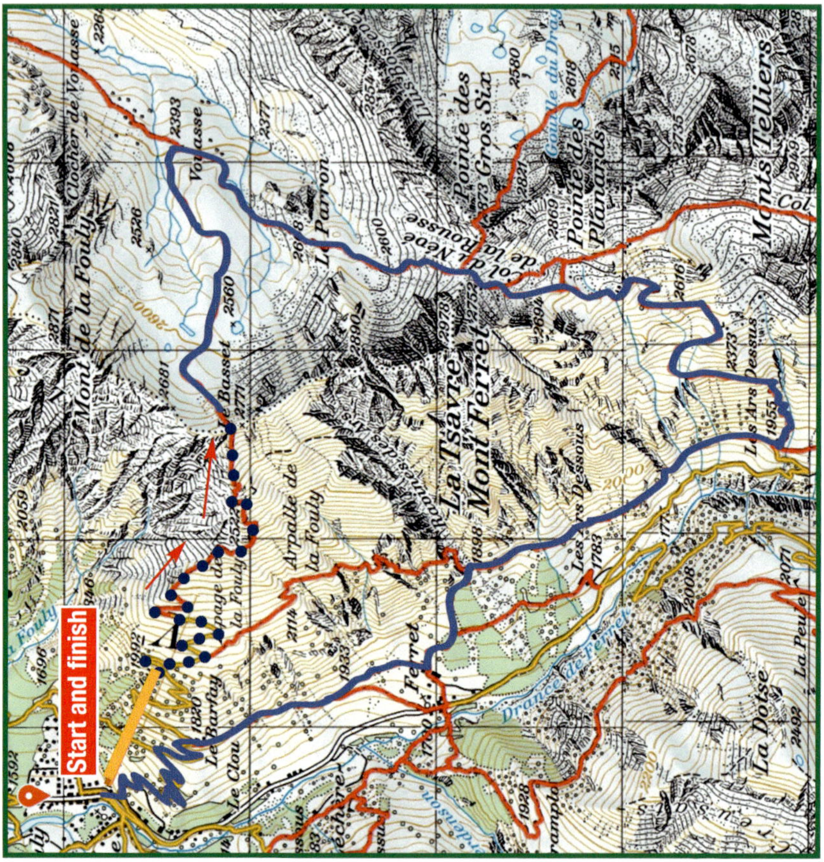

Altitude: 2,771 m
Level: Hiker
Time: 2 hours up + 1 hour 15 min down
Elevation: 1,900 m to 2,771 m
Map: Pays du Mont Blanc hiking map at 1/50 000, A1 edition and Swiss map 5003
Access: La Fouly parking lot in front of the Glaciers auberge.
From Chamonix, head towards Argentière (N 506) and cross the Swiss border towards Col de Forclaz. Go all the way to Martigny and then to the right take Grand-Saint-Bernard road. Take a right towards Orcières, then a right towards La Fouly, Val Ferret. It should take about 1h30. http://www.lafouly.ch

40 | Col du Basset (La Fouly)

A steep climb up to Col du Basset pass with plenty of Edelweiss flowers along the way. View of Mont Dolent and the A Neuve glacial basin as well as the Col Ferret along the entire climb (if you just turn around). At the pass there's a superb view of the Combe de l'A and the Grand Combin (when it's not covered with clouds!)

Take the mechanical chairlift from La Fouly (l'Arpalle). It will take you up 300 m (http://www.telelafouly.ch/fr)

Be warned– the chairlift only runs during the first 15 min of each hour from 8am to 4pm in July / August, and only during good weather (add 1h20 to your trip if you don't take the chairlift).

I would discourage you from taking this hike after a rain– it becomes a damp and slippery path. Once up the chairlift, head to the left and then go up a bit. Take the path towards the Col du Basset, Combe de l'A, marked white and red (you'll pass a trail to your right that heads towards Ars Dessus and Plan de la Chaux). The path heads steeply uphill all the way up to the pass. In the beginning, it heads through Alpine pastures with sheep.

After about 1 hour, you'll start to see the first Edelweiss flowers, which will be more and more numerous as you go along.

Some passageways are equipped with chains, which are mainly there to keep you from slipping. Don't be like me and, following poor instructions, go back down via the same route. Pick up a hiking map at the Fouly Office of Tourism (to the right of the chairlift) and you'll see that from the Col du Basset pass you can make a loop to return to La Fouly in 3 hours. The trail descends through the Combe de l'A Valley (2,600 m). Take a right towards the Col du Névé de la Rousse pass (2,752 m) and then head directly down to the Ars Dessus via a trail to your right. At Ars Dessus, take the Bergers trail along the right bank of the Dranse River.

All in all, this circular hike should take about 5 hours from the top of the chairlift.

Swiss mountainside

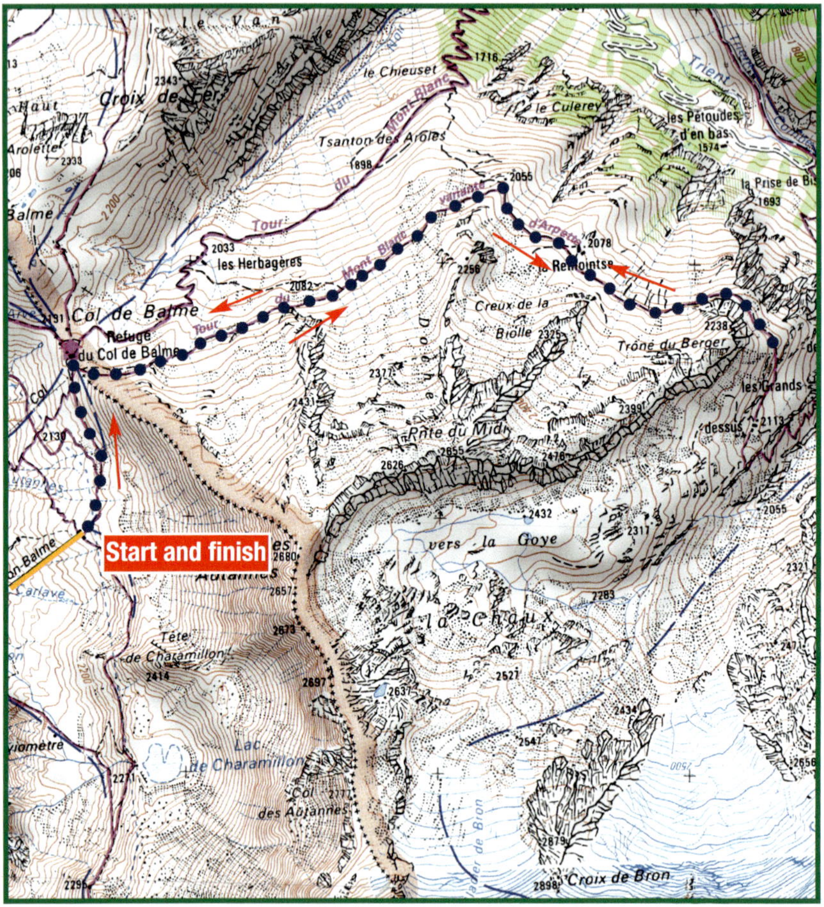

Altitude: 2,113 m
Level: Hiker
Time: 3 hours 30 min
Elevation: Elevated pathway
Map: IGN 3630
Access: Parking lot for the Charamillon cable car in the village of Tour.
After Argentière (N 506), while heading towards Col des Montets, you'll take almost immediately a little road on your right towards Tour.

41 I Cabane des Grands (from the Col de Balme pass)

A little known and rarely traveled hike to the Swiss Cabane des Grands (Grands Cabin), at the foot of the Grands glacier. On the elevated path amid rhododendrons, you'll overlook the village of Trient and discover the Trient and Grands glaciers.

Get a round-trip ticket for the Charamillon cable car + Autannes chairlift.
Once at the top of the chairlift (2,186 m), take the road to your left towards the Col de Balme (2,191 m). The Col de Balme pass marks the French-Swiss border. The Balme refuge, which is already visible, is a few minutes above the chairlift arrival station. Enjoy the view of Mont Blanc from a different angle.
At the Col de Balme pass, take the trail heading furthest to the right of the mountainside, towards Les Grands. (The time is incorrectly marked 1h10. It's an elevated trail so the time it takes to get there and back should be the same.) This trail is also a variation of the TMB.

The overhanging trail isn't very high up, but some areas are equipped with chains to cross over rocky projections.
At the beginning, there may be some snowy patches that you can go around instead of crossing.
After a slight descent, the trail bends to the right amid rhododendrons. In the first half of the journey, you'll pass the TMB pathway from Col de Balme to Trient and a continuous view over the village of Trient and the Col de la Forclaz pass.
In the last third of the journey, you'll have a view of the Trient glacier. Then, just before the journey ends, you'll see a Swiss cabin below you and the Grands glacier to the right.
For several minutes, follow the trail under the cabin (the trail that meets up with the Trient Chalet du Glacier in 50 min and the village of Trient or the Col de la Forclaz in 1h40) until you reach the cross. Then take the passage cut out of the rock. Turn around for a beautiful photo!
Go back the way you came and picnic at the cabin where the view is superb over both the Trient and Grands glaciers and, on the horizon, the Fenêtre d'Arpette.
For the way back, take the same trail backwards until you reach the Col de Balme pass. Then meet back up with the Autannes chairlift.

Swiss mountainside

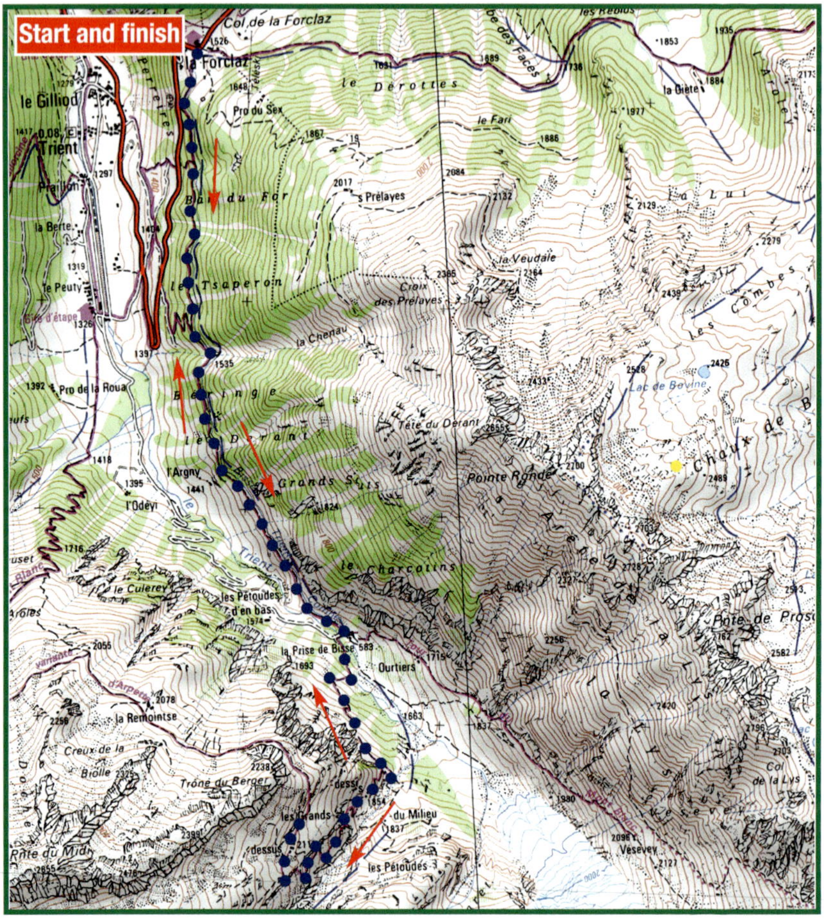

Altitude: 2,113 m
Level: Hiker
Time: 2 hours 15 min up + 1hour 45 min back
Elevation: 1,526 m to 2,113 m
Map: IGN 3630 OT
Access: Col de la Forclaz parking lot
Head towards Vallorcine (N506) and, after Argentière and Col des Montets pass, cross the Swiss border and then go up to the pass.

42 I Cabane des Grands (from le Col de La Forclaz)

A hike to the Swiss Cabane des Grands (Grands Cabin), at the foot of the Grands glacier. As the pathway runs alongside irrigation channels, you'll look over the village of Trient and then discover the Trient and Grands glaciers.

This hike allows you to reach Cabane Trient (the Trient cabin) without taking the mechanical lifts at Tour (see Hike 41). The way is well marked from the start at the Col de la Forclaz pass, on the right when you get to Chamonix.

From the pass to the Glacier chalet (50 min) the trail is flat and borders the Trient channel, overhanging the village of Trient and its pink church. To the right on the other side of the river, you'll see the Col de Balme pass.

In about 45 min, just before you get to the Glacier chalet, you'll reach a fork to the right leading towards Col de Balme and the Cabane des Grands. Go to the right and cross the wooden footbridge over the river– beautiful view of the glacier from this footbridge. The Glacier once reached all the way to the foot of the chalet, but has receded significantly in recent years.

After having crossed the footbridge, take a left towards Cabane Trient. Head up the river along the left bank through the half-shade, half-sun forest with the Trient glacier in front of you. The climb is rather steady.

Once you are 30 min from the footbridge, you'll pass a trail to the left that heads towards the Alpine pastures of Pétoncles. Continue your climb straight ahead along the side of the cliff. Soon after, you'll see the Grands glacier. The trail continues through a wild landscape and then, in just over 2 hours, you'll reach the foot of a passageway carved out of the cliff. One more turn and you'll see the cabin below you. Picnic at the cabin where the view is superb over both the Trient and Grands glaciers and, on the horizon, the Fenêtre d'Arpette.

For the way back, take the same trail as you did on the way there. In 30 min you'll reach the fork at the Alpine pastures de Pétoncles and in 1 hour you'll reach the footbridge at the Glaciers chalet. While heading back to the Col de la Forclaz pass, you can take the time to read the informational panels about the channels, the history of the Trient glacier and the exploitation of ice. You can also hike this route from the village of Trient. From the Le Peuty parking lot (1,326 m) at the end of the little road, it will take 1 hour to get back to the Glaciers chalet.

It will take about 6 hours to do the Le Peuty – Col de Balme loop, First Col de Balme (2h30), then Col de Balme-Cabane des Grands (see Hike 41), and then Cabane des Grands-Le Peuty.

Italian mountainside

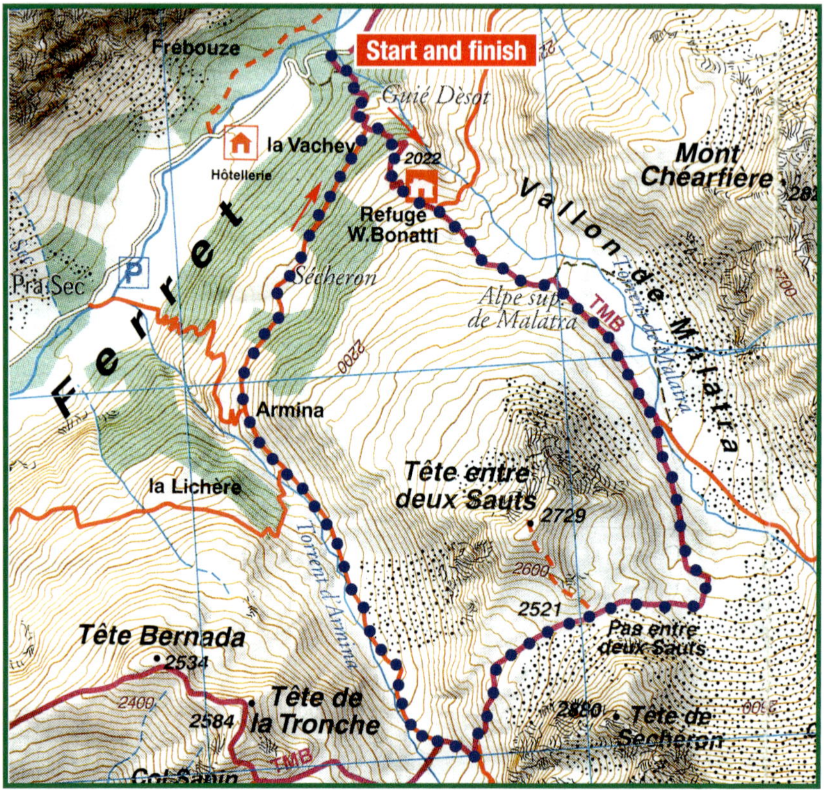

Altitude: 2,521 m
Level: Hiker
Schedule: 4 hours 30 min for the loop
Elevation: 1,680 m to 2,521 m
Map: Pays du Mont-Blanc hiking map (A1, Rando Editions)
Acces: Malatra Parking in Italy
From Chamonix, take the Mont-Blanc tunnel. At the end of the tunnel, turn left towards Entrêves-La Palud-Val Ferret, pass Planpincieux then park just before the hamlet of La Vachey at the level of the Malatra stream; allow 30 minutes minimum (26 km) but the travel time can greatly vary depending on the traffic in the Mont-Blanc tunnel and on the narrow road of the Val Ferret.

43 I Entre-Deux-Sauts

The Val Ferret is just minutes from the exit of the Mont-Blanc tunnel. This hike goes through wild landscapes, with a remarkable view on the southern Italian side of the Mont-Blanc range Val Ferret side.

The start of the hike can be a bit hard to find, the signs in Italy are less well marked than on the French side.
The first step is to reach the Bonatti refuge (2,022 m) which you will reach in less than an hour.

To do this, take the stone path to the right of the Malatra stream (left bank) that winds through a larch forest. At the first junction, continue on your left towards the Bonatti refuge. On leaving the forest floor, carry on through the meadows before reaching the refuge situated opposite the Grandes Jorasses. From the shelter, continue towards the alpine huts of the Alpe Superior of Malatra following the TMB trail from now on.
The trail climbs slowly across the meadows to the Col de Pas-Entre-Deux-Sauts (2,521 m) that you will reach in less than 3 hours. The hike is in the wilderness with an unusual view of the Italian mountainside of the Mont-Blanc.
You can picnic at the pass if it is not too windy.
From the Col de Pas-Entre-Deux-Sauts, you can do the roundtrip hike in an hour, using a slightly steep and precipitous path to the Tête-Entre-Deux-Sauts gazebo (2,729 m), that reveals the entire Italian side of the Mont-Blanc from the peaks of Miage to Mont-Dolent.
Start the descent still using the TMB. At a junction just before the torrent of Armina, you will leave the TMB to walk along the right bank of the torrent (so do not cross the stream). At each intersection encountered, always follow the path on the right. At the level of the Armina cabins that can be seen below, the view of Mont-Blanc on the Italian side is beautiful, a picture postcard with high snow-capped peaks dominating the Italian Val Ferret in the background.
Keep straight ahead to the Sécheron cabins, then go through the forest to join the stony trail used in the morning. Turn left, to reach the parking lot.
On the return, it is worthwhile to make a detour through the renowned and touristic "village" of Courmayeur, to enjoy, among other things, an excellent Italian ice-cream.

Tour of the Mont-Blanc

The legendary hike in the Alps that crosses three countries and which offers three different slopes of the Mont-Blanc mountain range: France and its glaciers, Italy and its rock faces, Switzerland and its pastures.

Nowadays, there are a vast number of ways to make ones "Tour du Mont-Blanc". Whatever option you choose, the TMB is for experienced hikers in good physical shape, given the uneven ground, the hiking time and the sequence of hiking days. The actual hiking time is on average 6 hours per day, with an average elevation gain of 700 to 900 m.

The recommended period is from late June to early September for passable passes.
Purists will say that the TMB is done carrying the backpack, anticlockwise and in full in 9 to 12 days according to the stages and recovery days one allows (distance about 170 km with 10 km of elevation gain).
So you can organize your TMB alone and book your nights in shelters before departure or choose between the different suggestions organized by hiking agencies.
Programs vary according to:

- The period of 6 to 10 days (there are also U-turns north or south in 5 days).
- Types of accommodation (guarded refuge, holiday cottages or hotels with more comfort).
- With or without transfers to shorten certain stops less attractive and encourage access to the most remarkable sites.
- With or without carrying a backpack.

Most suggested Tours are performed anticlockwise. (France, Italy, Switzerland, France).
With the transport of your backpack by car from one stage to another, you only need to carry a light day pack, which changes your life (especially for people with back problems).
I am giving away "my" Tour du Mont-Blanc called "Comfort" done in six days in a clockwise direction (probably easier than the anticlockwise version) but with the backpack.

Day 1: Chamonix to Argentière via the Lac Blanc and the Lacs de Chézerys

Half a day's hike for the first day. One takes the Flégère cable car in Les Praz-de-Chamonix, then the "highway" route towards the Lac Blanc (2,352 m).

The Lac Blanc or inescapable hiking in Chamonix (and the world that goes with it). Postcard panoramic scenery of the Mont-Blanc range almost in its entirety: the Mont-Blanc, the Aiguille du Midi, the Mer de Glace, the Drus, the Tour and Argentière glaciers.

Ibex for sure on the way.

From the Lac Blanc, a long descent of 900 m through the Lacs de Chézerys then through the forest to Argentière, which will make the thighs of the least trained suffer the next day!

You can see hikes N° 2 and N° 3 for more information on the Lac Blanc or Lacs de Chézerys (even if the route is different).

Day 2: Trient to Champex via Bovine

A short transfer from Argentière allows you to reach the village of Trient in Switzerland.

The second day is refreshing and rural between larch forests and high mountain pastures.

From the Bovine Pastures, the view is panoramic on Martigny, the Swiss Valley and the Rhone Valley.

The evening stop is a quiet resort in the delightful site of the Champex alpine lake.

Nevertheless, a long and demanding day with 750 m ascent and 850 m descent.

You can view hike N° 22 which describes the route in reverse, from Champex to Col de Forclaz.

Day 3: Champex to La Fouly

A quiet day of recovery with only 3 hours of hiking and a low elevation of 450 m on uncommonly followed paths through valleys and waterfalls. La Fouly is a pretty Swiss chalets village. France, Italy and Switzerland meet at the Mont-Dolent summit overlooking the village.

Day 4: La Fouly to Arnuva via Col Ferret

The itinerary follows either the classic tour of the Grand Col Ferret (2,537 m), or a less followed variation by the Petit Col Ferret (2,490m), these passes mark the border between Switzerland and Italy. Stunning views of the Swiss and Italian Val Ferret.
The climb through alpine pastures and herds of sheep leads to a pass that gives access to the gully "Combe des Fonds". View of the Dolent glacier. The climb continues along the stream that runs through the gully, up to a snowfield that heralds the "Petit Col Ferret". The trail then goes down to Arnuva the Italian Val Ferret via the Elena refuge and its alpine meadows (2,062 m).
Another beautiful elevation for this day, ascent 950 m and descent 900 m, under the gaze of glaciers and the Jorasses.
From Arnuva, you take a shuttle to join Courmayeur.
You get there early enough to enjoy the famous and touristic "village" of Courmayeur and enjoy an excellent Italian ice-cream among other things.

Day 5: Cantine de la Visaille to Chapieux via the Col de La Seigne and Ville-des-Glaciers

A short transfer from Courmayeur allows one to reach Cantine de la Visaille in the Italian Val Vény, at the foot of the Miage glacier.

After crossing the Arp Vieille bridge, one crosses the marshy meadow of the Combal plateau, then one climbs up sharp bends to the Elisabetta Soldini refuge (2,195 m).

Climb to the Col de La Seigne (2,516m) which marks the return to France, with superb views on the Italian side of Mont-Blanc.

Then a long descent to the remote valley of Chapieux (1,549 m) via Ville-des-Glaciers.

A day with an elevation gain of 950 m and 900 m downhill.

Day 6: Les Chapieux to Notre-Dame-de-la-Gorge via the Col du Bonhomme

Another lovely elevation for this final day, 900 m ascent up to the Croix du Col du Bonhomme refuge (2,433 m) with views of the Beaufortain and Tarentaise.

A long descent of 1,200 m to Notre-Dame-de-La-Gorge and its baroque chapel in the Contamines-Montjoie valley.

A transfer from Notre-Dame-de-La-Gorge brings you back to the station of Saint-Gervais-le-Fayet.

THE GLACIAL HIKES

To be done with a high-altitude mountain guide

Two criteria are taken into account in assessing the difficulty of a mountain hike: The general difficulty of the hike (Welzenbach scale) which takes into account the inclination of the snow slope and/or the difficulty of the rock climbing passages (6 levels from Easy to Extremely Difficult).
F (Easy): Snow Slopes up to 30°; short rock passages from 2 to 3.
PD (A Little Difficult): Slopes with snow up to 50°; rocky passages from levels 3 to 4.
These hikes are classified as « easy F » and « PD a little difficult » on the Welzenbach scale. This does not at all mean that they are accessible to all. The efforts made in the mountains, particularly above 3,000 m, require a top physical condition and a capacity to recover from hikes over several days.
The commitment expressed in Roman numerals on a scale of I to VII reflects a combination of factors characterizing an ascent: its length, its isolation, altitude, potential hazards such as rock falls or séracs…
Level I: the hike is done in 3 hours maximum, it is easy to stop the ascent, a fall would normally be without serious consequences.
Level II: the duration and effort of this climb can be up to 5 hours, in some areas there are possibilities of withdrawal, the consequences of a fall could be serious during short passages or under certain conditions.
These hikes are classified Level I and II.
Equipment needed (rental in sports shops): crampon walking shoes, crampons, harness, snap link, helmet, ice axe, telescopic sticks (the guide provides the ropes).

Glacial Hike

Altitude: 3,842 m Aiguille du Midi
Level: Glacial hike to be done with a guide
Schedule: Half-day with about 2 hours 30 min walking time
Elevation: Descent 650 m, Ascent 350 m
IGN map 3630 OT
Access: Aiguille du Midi-Chamonix cable car.

Haute Vallée Blanche Crossing

For all experienced hikers in good physical condition this is a magnificent glacier crossing from the Aiguille du Midi to the tip of Helbronner in Italy. The Return is via the scenic gondola of the Vallée Blanche. To be made on a fine day.

One must not have problems of vertigo because at the exit of the Aiguille du Midi cable car, one must descend the famous ridge of the Aiguille du Midi, which is not equipped with ropes in the summer. Although the crossing is not long, about 2h30, altitude must be reckoned with, so preferably to be done after a few more traditional hikes at lower altitudes.
Finally, after going down 2/3 of the course, there are two steep climbs with < 30° to reach the tip of Helbronner.

A big half day organized hike, starting at 7:30 am at the Aiguille du Midi cable car, you reach the summit 20 minutes later. It will be 8:30 am by the time you equip (crampons, ropes) at the end of the tunnel and go down the ridge. At 11 am, you'll be at the tip of Helbronner. Enjoy the view on the Italian side of the Matterhorn and Monte Rosa. By the time you catch a cable car for the return, you arrive at around 12:30 pm at the Aiguille du Midi. Once again take advantage of this superb vantage point of 360° on the summits of the Mont-Blanc from the different terraces, before going down into the valley.
You can have a late picnic stop at Plan de l'Aiguille, which is the first section of the cable car (Lac Vert 15 minutes) before descending to Chamonix.
After descending the ridge of the Aiguille du Midi, one goes down the high basin water supply of the Mer de Glace glacier formed by the Glacier du Géant. On the right, Cosmiques refuge, Mont-Blanc du Tacul and its line of hikers.
On the left you ignore the slope used in winter for skiing down the Vallée Blanche towards the Requin refuge.
One progresses to the tip of Helbronner; on the left, the Dent du Géant and the Grandes Jorasses.

Glacial Hike

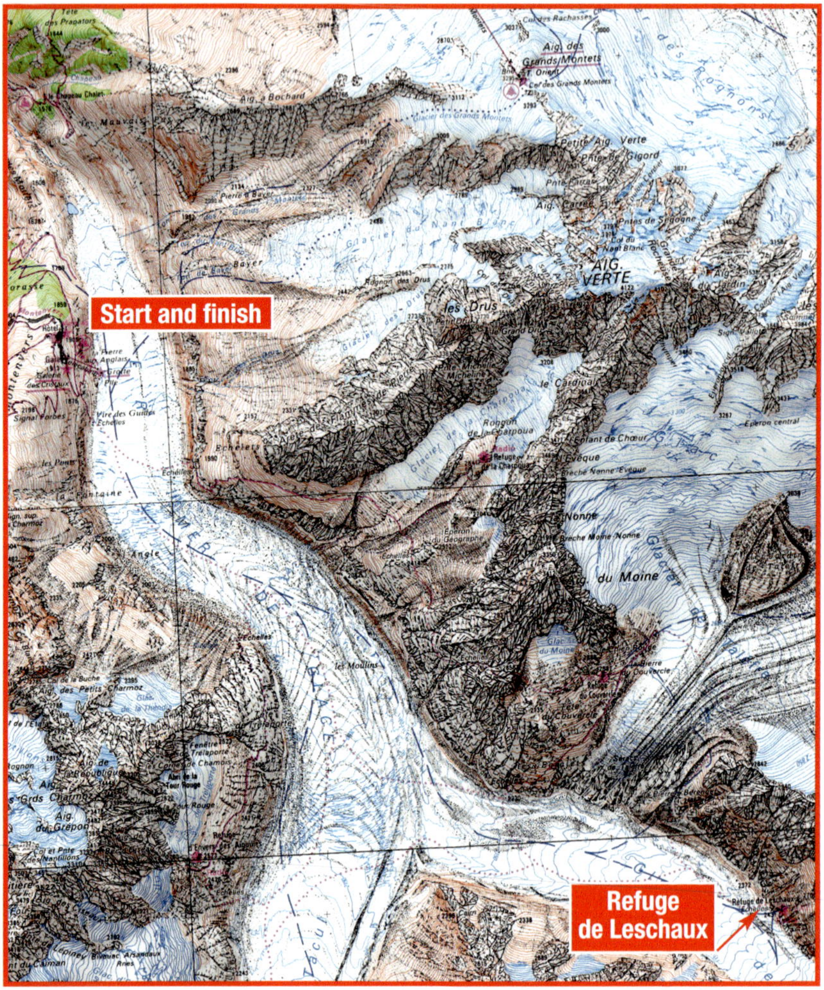

Altitude: 2,431 m Leschaux Refuge
Level: Glacial hike to be done with a guide
Schedule: One Day
IGN map 3630 OT
Access: Parking of Montenvers station in Chamonix

Refuge de Leschaux

For all experienced hikers and not subject to vertigo (downhill and climbing ladders), a great and magical day with a magnificent course on glaciers and in the background the Grandes Jorasses.

Take the train at Crémaillère that takes you to the top station of Montenvers (1,913 m) in 20 minutes. Head for the start of the ladders that overhang the Mer de Glace by 250 meters, following the retreat of the glaciers.

Do not hesitate to make sure the guide belays you for the descent of the ladders which is impressive the first time. Shortly after joining the moraine on the left bank of the glacier, the guide will make you put on the crampons depending on the weather. Nothing complicated in glacier walking with crampons on slopes of < 30°.

Then you go back up the tip of the Mer de Glace. The climb occurs amidst the crevasses.

After about two hours, you leave the Tacul Glacier on the right and proceed towards the Leschaux Glacier.

If you are lucky, you might see a herd of chamois whilst you climb up the Leschaux Glacier. Failing that, you can pick up a few pieces of quartz, smoked if possible!

Ignore on your left the ladders leading "directly" to the Couvercle refuge. Continue the ascent of the glacier with the North Face of the Grandes Jorasses in the background. After 3h30 you reach the foot of very steep ladders and the refuge in 4 hours.

After a short pause at the Leschaux refuge facing the Grandes Jorasses, you return by the same route in approximately 3 hours.

You get to the upper station of Montenvers after climbing the ladders.

Glacial Hike

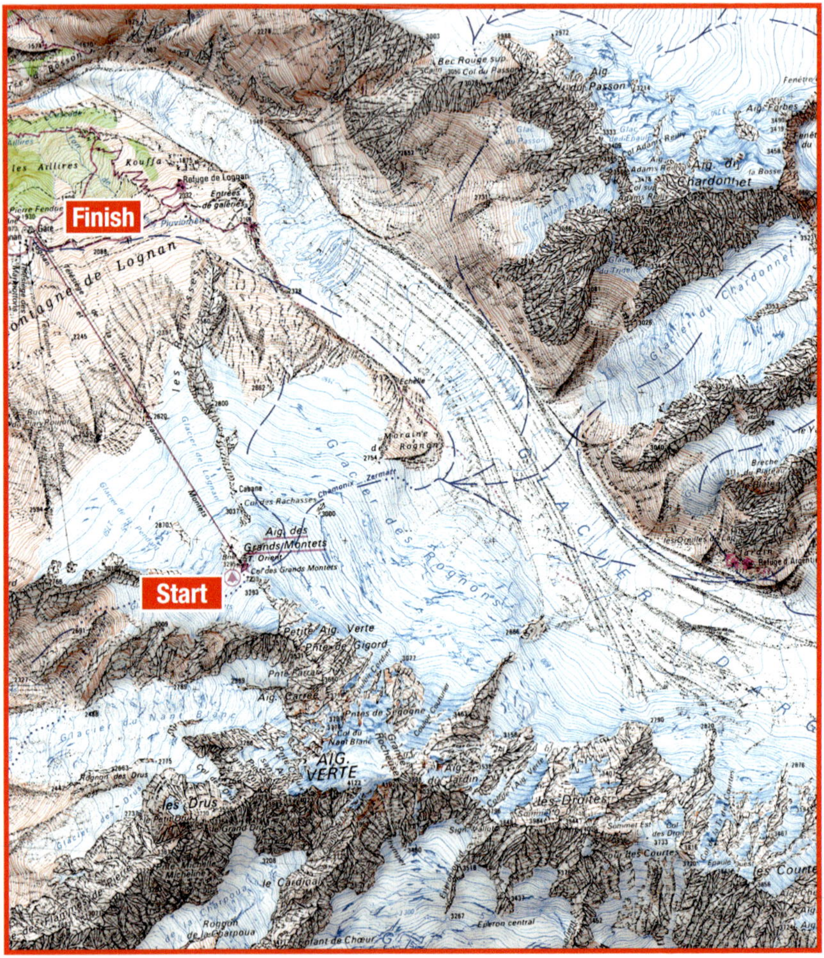

Altitude: 2,771 m Argentière Refuge
Level: Glacial hike to be done with a guide
Schedule: One Day
Gain: Grands Montets (3,295 m) to Lognan (1,973 m)
IGN map 3630 OT
Access: Grands Montets cable car in Argentière.

Refuge d'Argentière

For all experienced hikers, a long downhill glacial hike on the Rognons and Argentière glaciers. The Argentière glacier, between its two mythically named walls of peaks, offers a view of Mont-Dolent. To be done on a fine day.

Organized one day hike. Starting with the first cable car at 7:30 am at the Grands Montets. Picnic at the refuge. This long hike down of about 7 km could make your thighs hurt the next day for the least trained! Do not forget your sticks!
One can also get to the Argentière refuge in a day round-trip from the mid-point station of Croix de Lognan (3h30 of climbing from Croix de Lognan to the refuge and then 2h30 to go back down).
Take advantage of the panoramic indicator and the 360° view once you get to the arrival station of the Grands-Montets before getting equipped at the bottom of the metal stairs.

The hike starts on a steep downhill slope and continues to cross the Rognons glacier from the Col des Grands Montets.
At the foot of the Argentière glacier, the guide will make you remove the crampons or not to progress across this portion of the glacier which is not too steep. You reach the moraine opposite, on the right bank of the glacier. From there, an uphill trail (a little hard for an end of morning hike) leads to the Argentière refuge where one can picnic. On the roof of the shelter nestled in granite, a motorcycle was dropped by a helicopter, the keeper being an enthusiast.
Enjoy the view on the peaks, on the left bank of the glacier "Les Courtes, Les Droites, La Verte" and on the right bank "Aiguilles du Chardonnet and Argentière, Tour Noir".
The Cable car's schedule for the last one at Lognan (5 pm) unfortunately leaves little time at the refuge, (friendly service, you can have lunch there) because you need to have a safety margin if you do not want to add 2 hours to reach Argentière from Lognan if you miss the last cable car!
The descent from the refuge (about 2h30) follows the same route in crossing the glacier to the moraine's left bank which you will have to go back up to reach an overhanging trail on rocks overlooking the glacier. You will reach the top of ladders (70 m) which you will use to go down. At the foot of the ladder, follow the edge of the moraine and the flat of the glacier to the "Viewpoint" where one crosses many hikers who come to watch the séracs waterfalls and the glacier's crevasses. Then join a dirt road, below which you see the Chalet-Refuge of Lognan, leading to the mid-point cable station of Grands Montets.

Glacial Hike

Altitude: 1,913 to 2,687 m
Level: Glacial hike to be done with a guide
Schedule: 3 days, 2 nights in a refuge
IGN map 3630 OT
Access: Train Station parking at Montenvers in Chamonix

Tour de la Mer de Glace

For all experienced hikers and not suffering from vertigo, a magnificent course, unforgettable and timeless. Dotted with ladders to climb from glaciers to shelters and vice versa, this route takes you into the heart of the Mont-Blanc mountain range and its silent vastness.

Organized 3-day hiking trek

Day 1: Refuge du Requin (2,516 m)

Take the rack-train that takes you to the Montenvers upper station (1,913 m) in 20 minutes. Head for the start of the ladders, 250 meters overlooking the Mer de Glace. Do not hesitate to make sure the guide belays you going down the ladders which is impressive for a first time.

Shortly after joining the moraine on the left bank of the glacier, you put on crampons for an introduction to glacier walking. Nothing fancy on slopes < 30°. After this first experience and depending on weather, the guide will make you remove your crampons, which is surprising at first.

You then go back up the tip of the Mer de Glace toward the Shark refuge.

You go back up amidst the crevasses. After about two hours, you leave on the left the Leschaux glacier and proceed toward the Tacul glacier which supplies the Mer de Glace. On the top right hand side you can see the Envers de l'Aiguille refuge where the glacier becomes flatter.

You progress on the glacier, you reach the glacier's moraine on the left bank then you climb up the rock face leading to the refuge, firstly by metal ladders then finally by a path.

You arrive at the Requin refuge in the middle of the afternoon (4 hours of actual walking). The site is magical of course. The refuge is perched on a headland overlooking the Glacier du Geant's séracs, its famous "Salle à manger" (Dining Room).

The refuge is mostly visited in winter and in spring, which is a stop and a pause from the ski descent of the Vallée Blanche from the Aiguille du Midi. Dinner and overnight stay at the refuge (60 beds).

Day 2: Refuge du Requin to the Refuge du Couvercle (2,687m) via the Refuge de Leschaux (2,450m)

Early in the morning, you will start by going down the ladders taken the day before to reach the glacier. Then back down the Tacul glacier to the junction where Leschaux glacier comes from the right.

Going up the Leschaux glacier, you might be lucky to see a herd of chamois. Otherwise, pick up a few pieces of quartz, smoked if possible!

Ignore to the left the ladders leading "directly" to the Couvercle refuge.

You continue to climb the glacier with, in the background, the North Face of the Grandes Jorasses.

Picnic on the glacier before once again taking on a steep climb of ladders to the Leschaux refuge.

After a break at Leschaux facing the majestic Grandes Jorasses, the hike continues through a rocky trail to the Talèfre glacier that must be crossed before tackling the steep path which joins the Couvercle refuge.

A great day, in a magical place, where the view embraces both Mont-Blanc and the Grandes Jorasses.

Dinner and overnight stay at the shelter (120 beds).

Day 3: Return to Montenvers

The return to the top station of Montenvers is made via an overhead balcony footpath overlooking the Aiguilles de Chamonix and the Mer de Glace. Very little walking on the glacier for this last day, except to reach the bottom of the ladders used the first day which will have to be climbed up. In theory, you are "vaccinated" after all this going up and down ladders, so you should be able to tackle this final ascent with confidence (250 m nonetheless) !

Arrival in Chamonix mid-afternoon.

Glacial Hike

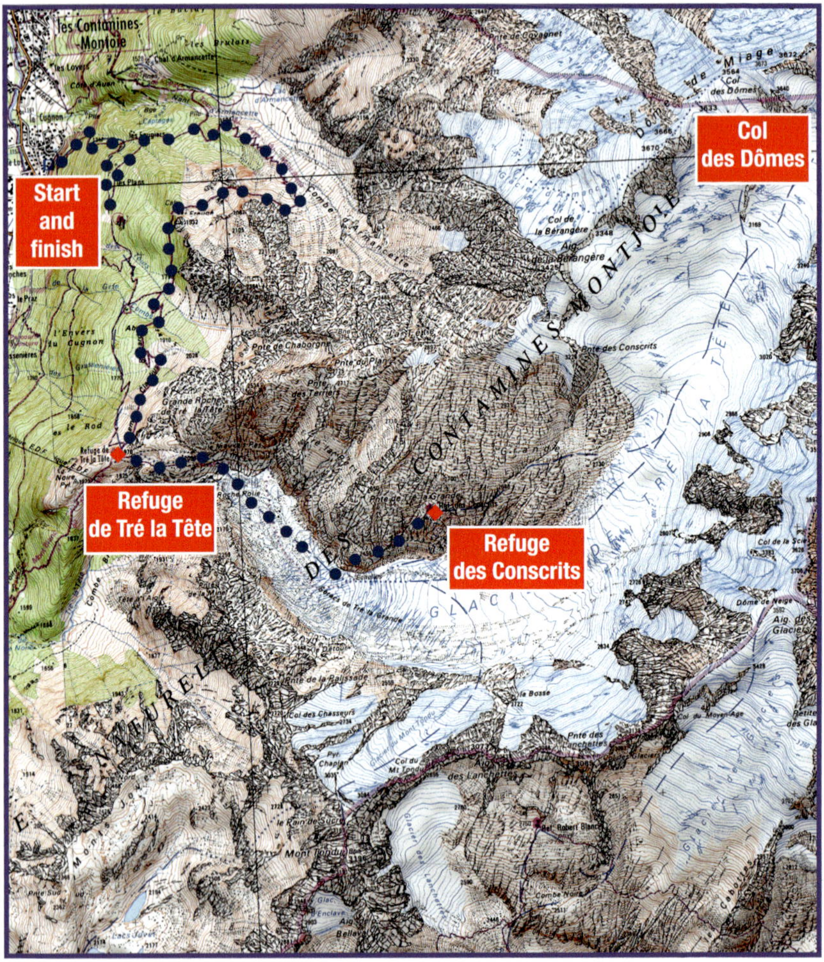

Altitude: 3,633 m
Level: Glacial hiking, guide required
Time: 2 days, 1 night at a refuge
Elevation: Hameau du Cugnon (1,256 m) to the 3rd peak (3,633 m)
Map: IGN 3531 ET
Access: Hameau de Cugnon at the Contamines-Montjoie exit

Dômes de Miage, central summit

For experienced hikers only! You'll need to be in excellent physical shape. The first day is exhausting (1,600 m increase in altitude) and the night at the refuge is short (wake-up at 3:30am). The second day is demanding in terms of length (11 hours minimum), the increase in elevation (1,030 m) and the descent (2,400 m decrease in elevation).
The first day is dedicated to climbing up to the Conscrits refuge (2,601 m) passing by the Tré-la-Tête chalet-hotel (1,967 m).
The second day, the climb up to the 3rd peak of the Dômes de Miage allows you to take on the Val Montjoie and contemplate the mythical ridge of the Dômes de Miage, the Italian side of Mont Blanc, and the Bionnassay ridge.

2-day organized hike

Day 1: Hameau du Cugnon (1,256 m) to the Conscrits refuge (2,601 m), about 5 h 30 min of hiking

From the Hameau du Cugnon parking lot, you'll reach the Tré-la-Tête chalet-hotel for a picnic in about 2h20. Many trails lead there, and all of them initially head up through a beautiful forest. At the first intersection, I suggest you take the trail to the left. At the second intersection, take the one marked "Les Plans," as it will give you some gorgeous views over the Contamines-Montjoie Valley or Val Montjoie.

In the early afternoon, you'll leave from the Conscrits refuge, which you should reach in around 2h45.

A long, aerial footbridge will soon be put in place 56 meters above a large gorge, allowing you to stick to your schedule without rolling up your sleeves in the summer! It will also allow experienced hikers to reach the Conscrits refuge by themselves. Alas– it wasn't yet in place when I did this hike.

At first you'll take a hiking trail leading to a place called "Le Mauvais Pas," which is a view over the glacial basin, or rather the glacial moraine. After a short descent, the trail comes to an end at the final strip of the Tré-la-Tête glacier, entirely covered in rocks at this location. Then you'll head up the moraine (rather unpleasant, like all moraines) without equipment, following the stone cairns. Next you'll have to roll up your sleeves and rope up to reach the right bank of the glacier.

Next, depending on your guides, some will have you take the ladders (to be removed once the footbridge is put in place) or climb up a steeper slope of the glacier. One last, very steep trail will allow you to reach the Conscrits refuge, which overlooks the Tré-la-Tête glacier's long strip.

It's a beautiful refuge (capacity: 94) with comfortable, mixed dormitories, heartwarming food, and charming hospitality.

Day 2: Summit of the 3rd Peak of the Dômes de Miage, long descent via the Tré-la-Tête glacier

Departure around 4:15am. Following an uphill trail, in a little over 1 hour you'll reach the edge of the glacier where you'll have to roll up your sleeves. You'll head up the glacier towards Col de l'Infranchissable, with a view of the Italian side of Mont Blanc all along the climb.
The slope then flattens out as it heads towards Col des Dômes, between the 3rd and 4th peaks. Val-Montjoie will be at your feet and, behind you, the Aiguille de Bionnassay. After one last steep slope, you'll reach the central summit of the Dômes de Miage. The Dômes de Miage is composed of five mountain peaks that stretch out over more than 3 km. From the summit of the 3rd peak, you'll have a superb view over the famous aerial arête, the departure point for crossing the last two snowy peaks on the way to the Aiguille de la Bérangère.
Depending on the guides, you can either descend on the same path, with a quick snack break at the Conscrits refuge, or entirely via the uneven Tré-la-Tête glacier (without passing by the refuge), between crevices and snow bridges.
It should take about 1h30 from the Tré-la-Tête chalet-hotel de to the Cugnon parking lot.
One small regret: taking into account the length of the journey (on the 2nd day), you might as well do the loop and cross the Dômes de Miage all the way until the Aiguille de la Bérangère, which will take you to the Conscrits refuge (loop of 6-7 hours of walking + about 4 hours to descend back into the valley). If the length of the journey ends up being about the same, crossing the Dômes de Miage will be more technical in nature since it will require walking next to the void along the sharp arête and, during certain times, the snowy Bérangère slope that leads to the Conscrits refuge can be icy.

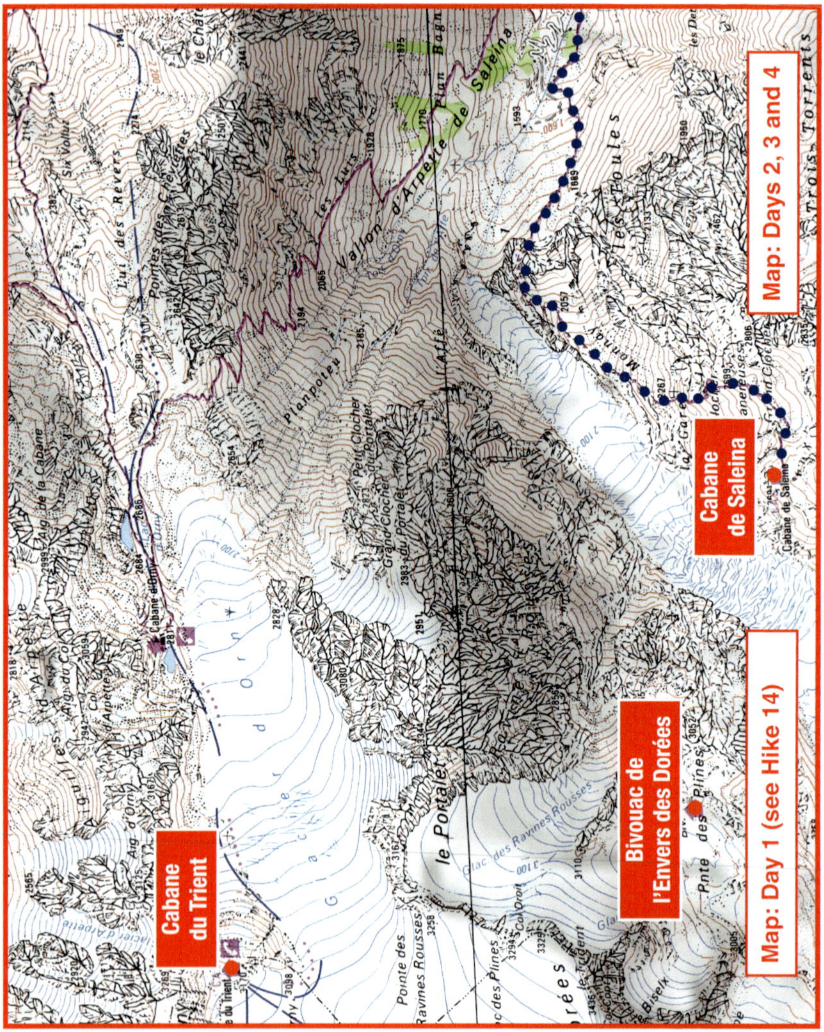

Altitude: between 2,185 m and 3,529 m
Level: Glacial hiking, guide required
Time: 4 days, 3 nights in a refuge
Access: Tour parking lot

The 3 Passes

Behind the well-traveled Tour and Trient glaciers, the Saleinaz glacial basin and cabin are a peaceful haven. It's a rich learning experience with a small rock climb and the chance to use many progression techniques on the glacier. There are also a variety of landscapes between glacial basins, minerals, and the hidden sides of well-known summits

4-day organized hike

Day 1 : Refuge Albert 1er (2,702 m)

In the early afternoon, take the Charamillon cable car and the Autannes chairlift (2,185 m). See Hike 14 from the Albert 1er refuge located on the right bank of the Tour glacier. You'll reach the refuge in 2 hours.
Room and board at the refuge (capacity: 148).

Day 2: Climb up to Aiguille du Tour (3,529 m) and Cabane Trient (3,170 m)

It will be a long day with departure at sunrise (6:30am) and arrival at Cabane Trient (the Trient cabin) around 4pm.

After 15 min walking along the trail leaving the refuge, it'll be time to roll up your sleeves and get strapped up. The climb up the Tour glacier to the upper Col du Tour (3289m) marks the French-Swiss border. You shouldn't have any particular difficulties as the slope is relatively easy going. You'll step foot on the Trient glacier.

The climb up to the Aiguille du Tour is not part of the standard 3 passes program. A snowy slope leads to the last 100 meters of rock climbing.

A particularly beautiful view of the Valais Alps and, in the distance, the summits of Grand-Combin, Cervin and Mont-Rose, among others.

On the way down rocky steps via the same route, you'll climb rapidly up to the Col du Tour pass for a picnic, safely disconnected.

In the afternoon, you'll cross the Trient plateau, overlooked by the Aiguilles Dorées, and reach Cabane Trient.

Room and board at the refuge (capacity: 128).

Day 3: Cabane Trient (3,170m) to Cabane Saleinaz (2,691m) in Switzerland

A short day departure at sunrise (6:30) and arrival at the cabin in time for lunch around 1:30pm

You'll climb up Trient glacier towards Col des Plines (another possibility is to climb by the Fenêtre de Saleinaz, depending on the snow). You'll descend from the Col des Plines along a steep slope. A long journey continues through the glacial moraine rocks and passes by the Envers des Dorées bivouac (2,985m). You'll reach the Saleinaz glacier and cross it this day without too much effort to reach the right bank. More rocks on the way to the trail that leads to Cabane Saleinaz (the Saleinaz cabin). Spend the afternoon in the sun contemplating the Saleinaz glacial basin, between the hidden sides of the Aiguille du Chardonnet and the Aiguille d'Argentière. On the other side, the Planereuse steeples watch over the cabin.

Room and board at the little-frequented refuge (capacity: 48). The cabin is guarded by volunteers who often offer tea to welcome in visitors.

Day 4 :

The last day (a big 8-hr day) of the 3 passes journey could not be carried out because the conditions were too dangerous this year. In principle, you head up the Saleinaz glacier to cross the Col des Planeureuses pass (3,050m). You then cross the Planeureuses glacier to get to the Col de Crête. Finally, you cross the little Treutse Bô glacier to reach the last pass, located at the foot of Grand Darey. A snowy 35° corridor lets you descend onto the A Neuve glacier. You'll reach Cabane A Neuve (A Neuve cabin) by descending along the left bank of the glacier, returning to La Fouly in Switzerland.

Instead, we descended directly down to Cabane Saleinaz by an Alpine trail that leads to Praz-de-Fort in the Swiss Val Ferret. It takes about 4 hours, of which around 45 min "corded up" to cross a rocky aerial passage equipped with chains, cables and steps over a vertical drop of about 200 m.

Arrival into a rural valley covered in old chalets of Alpine pasture.

Have a picnic and then return to the Tour parking lot by taxi.

Glacial Hike

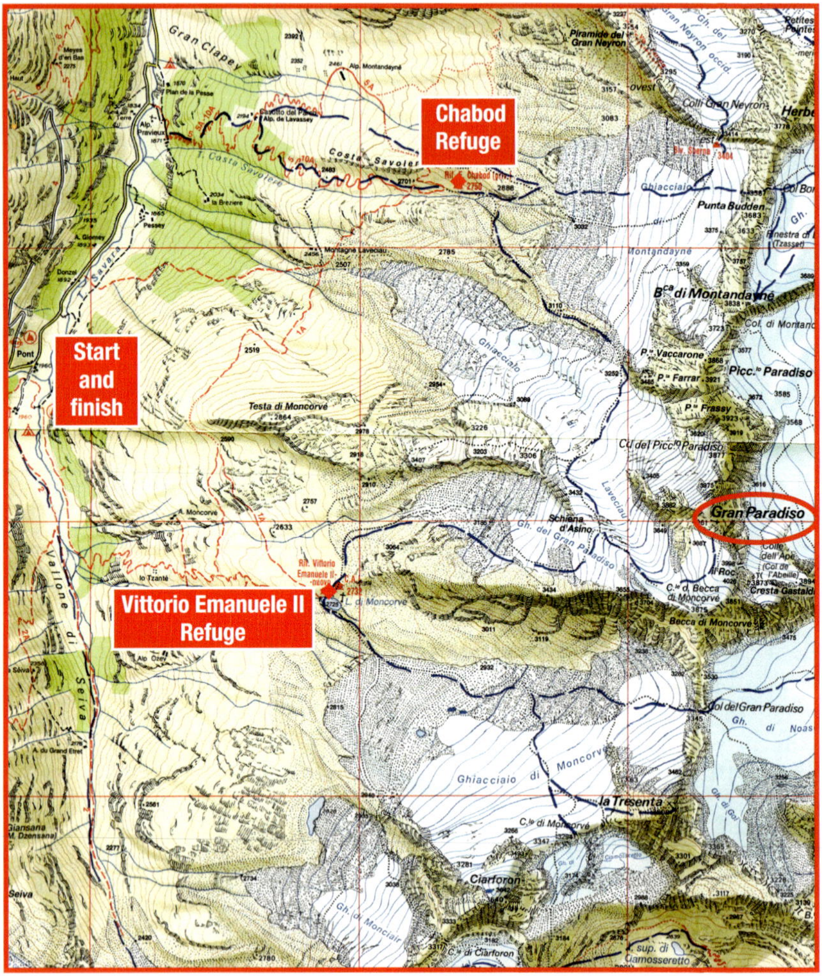

Altitude: between 1,960 m and 4,065 m
Level: Glacial hiking, guide required
Time: 3 days, 2 nights in a refuge
Access: Village de Pont (1,960 m) in Val d'Aoste, Italy, 1h30 from Chamonix via the Mont Blanc tunnel

Grand Paradis

For all experienced hikers, this is a 4,000 m hike in Val d'Aoste, Italy, known for being easy and not starting with mechanical lifts. The Grand Paradis is an exceptional gazebo over the Alps. Visit two refuges: Chabod and Vittorio Emanuele II.

3-day organized hike

The hike can also be done in 2 days with only one night at a refuge (either Chabod or Vittorio Emanuele II). Over 3 days, you give yourself more possibilities in case there is bad weather or strong winds and you avoid, the second day, an intense drop in elevation of 2,105 m coming out of a 10-hr walk.
Be careful– since you'll be leaving from 4,000 m up, even if it's summer you'll need to plan several layers of clothing to progressively cover up, and also for the climb on the 2nd day. I suggest a Gorex vest or something similar to protect you from the wind, often present at the Grand Paradis summit.

Day 1: Refuge Federico Chabod (2,750m). Elevation gain of 850 m in 2h30.

Leave from Chamonix around 10am. Arrive at Pravieux (a hamlet of Valsavaranche, 2 km before Village de Pont) around noon to picnic before climbing up to the Chabod refuge. The trail goes along the Old Royal Mule road, which climbs through larches before meeting with vast, flowered slopes. The refuge is situated at the foot of the northwest side of Grand Paradis, at the center of the Grand Paradis national park.
Room and board at the refuge (capacity: 85).

Day 2: Grand Paradis summit (4,065m) and descent to the Vittorio Emanuele II refuge (2,732 m).
1,315 m elevation gain in 5 hours, 1,333 m drop in elevation in 3 hours.

Nighttime departure around 5am. In about 1 hour you'll reach the final leg of the Laveciau glacier (3,252 m) where you'll have to roll up your sleeves. Climb up the barely cracked glacier until you get to the junction (3,750 m) with the Mont-Grand-Paradis glacier, which you'll take on the way down to reach the Vittorio Emanuele II refuge.

The slope is more constant when you head towards the Col de Becca di Moncorve pass (3,875 m), where the Gran Paradiso summit appears on the left. There's still a long journey ahead to reach the rocky, aerial arête where those who don't have vertigo can go see the statue of the Madonna poised at the summit. There are a few meters of aerial climbing on a narrow path over the void where you'll need to be attached to others to cross.

There's a beautiful 360° view over the summits, from the Pô plains to the Barre des Ecrins. If there are no clouds and someone can show you, you'll also see Mont Blanc, Grand Combin, Mont Rose, Cervin, and more.

Head back down to the Vittorio Emanuele II refuge via the Gran Paradiso glacier and its moraine, walking amid boulders. You'll reach the refuge around 1pm and a good plate of pasta will be there to comfort you.

The refuge is located at the foot of Trésenta, in the Grand Paradis national park. Room and board at the refuge (capacity: 150).

Day 3: Climb up Tresenta (3,609 m), or other hike depending on the time and participant fitness

Since Tresenta was pretty much just stone this year, the guides decided to suggest that we do an off-trail hike between the following moraines and glaciers: di Moncorve, di Monciair, del Breuil, and del Grant Etret. Leave at 6am and you'll see Grand Paradis from a different angle.

Arrive to the village of Pont at 11:30am, after having reached the very wild Vallone di Seiva trail that leads to the bottom of the valley by following the left bank of the Savara river. Enjoy a picnic on the terrace.

Arrival to Chamonix in the middle of the afternoon.

PRACTICAL TIPS

Warning

Doing the hikes in this guide is at your own risk. The hiker is responsible for the accident which he could be a victim of and should be well insured. Our liability shall in no way be engaged by your use of the information available to you.
The routes in this guide are for your information only, of which the aim is to suggest an interesting hike. The markers could have been modified since we made the last trek. Each hike has been specified with a level of difficulty. These are an indication only and it is up to the hiker to determine whether his physical condition and the external conditions (weather, soil conditions, etc..) enable him/her to undertake the hike.
The hiking period is generally the same as when shelters are kept, from mid-June to mid September. It still varies from one year to the next depending on snow conditions, so before leaving you have to make sure the chosen route is passable.

In the Mountain

• The rule of "leave early to come back early" will enable you to enjoy the scenery with the best light and without the clouds that often arrive in the early afternoon but also to ensure a safety margin for the time you need to respect.
• Weather conditions are very localized and change very fast. Always check the local weather before undertaking a hike. Always know how to adapt when unforeseen difficulties arise even if you have to give up the hike, and learn to recognize your limits.
• Take emergency numbers with you; be careful, as coverage of mobile phone networks is not complete.
• Whenever possible, inform someone of your route and estimated time of return.

Equipment

- A hiking map
- Walking shoes with rising stems to protect from ankle sprains
- A pair of telescopic walking sticks
- A backpack of 30 liters
- Clothing following the principle of three layers (including polar, wind breaker)
- Sunglasses, sunscreen, cap or hat
- Rain cape, woolly hat, light gloves
- Pocket knife, small aid kit, flashlight
- Camera
- 1.5 liters of water for a day hike
- Snack and energy snacks

USEFUL INFORMATION

Weather forecast

- **Weather forecast by Météo-France posted at the Maison de la Montagne and the Tourist Office in Chamonix Mont-Blanc**
- **Answering Machine**: 08 99 71 02 74

Mountain Rescue

- **High-Mountain Gendarmerie squad (PGHM):**
  04 50 53 16 89, www.pghm-chamonix.com
- **European emergency number:** 112 from cell phone

Mountain information

- **Maison de la Montagne and Office de Haute Montagne (OHM) in Chamonix:**
  04 50 53 22 08, www.ohm-chamonix.com
- **Aiguilles Rouges Nature Reserve: Chalet Montets Pass**
  04 50 54 02 24, www.rnaiguillesrouges.org

Tourism Offices

- **Chamonix:** 04 50 53 00 24, www.chamonix.com
- **Les Houches:** 04 50 55 50 62, www.leshouches.com
- **Servoz:** 04 50 47 21 68, www.servoz.com
- **Vallorcine:** 04 50 54 60 71, www.vallorcine.com
- **Saint Gervais:** 04 50 47 76 08, www.saintgervais.com
- **Passy Plaine Joux:** 04 50 58 80 52, www.passy-mont-blanc.com
- **Trient (Switzerland):** www.trient.ch
- **Champex (Switzerland):** +41 27 775 23 83, www.champex.ch
- **La Fouly (Switzerland):** +41 27 775 23 84, www.lafouly.ch
- **Courmayeur (Italy)**: www.courmayeurmontblanc.it

Transportation

- **Chamonix Bus :** 04 50 53 05 55, www.chamonix-bus.com
  Free shuttles with guest card
- **Chamonix SNCF station :** 04 50 78 45 60
- **Mont-Blanc Express Train**
  Saint-Gervais to Martigny (Switzerland), serves all the villages through Servoz, Les Houches, Chamonix, Argentière and Vallorcine, free from Servoz to Vallorcine with guest card
- **www.viamontblanc.com**
  This site provides all the information needed to move around the Mont-Blanc using public transport. You can download : maps, timetables and even get directions.
- **Mont-Blanc Tunnel :** 04 50 55 55 00, www.tunnelmb.net

Ski lifts

- **Compagnie du Mont-Blanc :**
  04 50 53 22 75, www.compagniedumontblanc.com
  The Compagnie du Mont-Blanc is the owner of most of the ski lifts in the valley. It offers a package "Mont-Blanc Multipass" which works like a ski pass.
  - Chamonix
    Plan de l'Aiguille – Aiguille du Midi – Helbronner
    Montenvers – Mer de Glace
    Planpraz – Brévent
    Flégère – Index
  - Argentière
    Lognan – Grands-Montets
  - Le Tour Vallorcine
    Charamillon-Col de Balme
    Télécabine Vallorcine
  - Les Bossons
    Télésiège

• Saint-Gervais-Le Fayet
  Tramway du Mont-Blanc (Le Fayet-Nid d'Aigle)

➢ **Les Houches :**
• Bellevue
• Le Prarion

Shelters

➢ **Association La Chamoniarde :** 04 50 53 22 08, www.chamoniarde.com
➢ **Le Nid d'Aigle, Tête Rousse, Le Goûter :** www.lesrefugesdumassifdumontblanc.fr

Mountain guides

➢ **Compagnies des guides de Chamonix :** 04 50 53 00 88, www.chamonix-guides.com
➢ **Association internationale des guides du Mont-Blanc :** 04 50 53 27 05, www.guides-du-montblanc.com
➢ **Maison des guides de Vallorcine :** 04 50 54 60 69, www.maisondelamontagne-vallorcine.fr
➢ **Odyssée Montagne à Servoz :** 04 50 91 20 83, www.odyssee.montagne.fr"

Hiking maps

➢ **Pays du Mont-Blanc, A1 - Rando-Editions, scale : 1 / 50 000**
➢ **Chamonix-Massif du Mont-Blanc, IGN – 3630 OT map, scale 1 / 25000**
➢ **St Gervais-Les-Bains – Massif du Mont-Blanc, IGN – 3531 ET map, scale 1 / 25 000**
➢ **Massif et tour du Mont-Blanc, Carte en Poche Libris, scale 1 / 25 000**

Miscellaneous

➢ **Free WiFi :** Tourism Office or Chamonix Media library
➢ **Website :** www.chamonix-randos.com

Achevé d'imprimer par
SARL ACBE - COPY MEDIA
33612 CANEJAN CEDEX
pour le compte des éditions Éditinter

Dépôt légal juin 2016
Imprimé en France

IMPRIM'VERT®